MARKER MAGIC

MARKER MAGIC

The Rendering Problem Solver for Designers

Richard M. McGarry
and
Greg Madsen

JOHN WILEY & SONS, INC.

New York   Chichester   Weinheim   Brisbane   Singapore   Toronto

Cover photograph by Ken Schiff.

Berol and Prismacolor are registered
trademarks of Berol Corporation

Library of Congress Cataloging-in-Publication Data:

McGarry, Richard M., 1948-
    Marker magic: the rendering problem solver for designers/
Richard M. McGarry, Greg Madsen.
        p.   cm.
    Includes index.
    ISBN 0-471-28434-3
    1. Architectural rendering.   2. Interior decoration rendering.
3. Dry marker drawing.   I. Madsen, Greg.   II. Title.
NA2726.3.M34   1992
    720'.28'4—dc20   92-6773

Printed in Hong Kong

10   9

For
Elizabeth Joanna Austin
(1922-1991)
We miss you.

ACKNOWLEDGMENTS

After graduation from art school, the authors launched on a quest: to educate the masses about good design. One thing that all those design courses had taught us was that there was an awful lot of bad design out there—and it was our job to fix it.

Armed with college degrees that certified our good taste and a collection of aphorisms that defined the design sensibilites of the early 1970s, such as "form follows function," "less is more," "beige goes with everything," and "Helvetica, used with imagination, is the only typeface you'll ever need," we asserted our concept of good design on every new client we acquired.

After years of battling with our customers and mumbling under our breath about their incredible lack of taste, however, we discovered three things:

■ "Form follows function" can be used to justify just about any design.

■ "Good design" is a moving target; fashions shift in architectural, interior, and graphic design almost as quickly as a couturier's hemlines.

■ Our clients are usually right.

We began to listen to and learn from our clients, instead of immediately foisting our concepts on them. Their comments and suggestions became something to look forward to.

Successful, opinionated clients can actually be a blessing because they expose you to the hidden criteria and insights that make it easier to create the truly brilliant design solutions. Their insistence that they receive something different, something better, will goad you on to refine your work one more time.

Each of the clients listed here has taught us at least one valuable lesson that has been incorporated in this book. We thank them all: Les Beilinson, Architect; Chris Belland, Old Town Key West Delvelopment; Tom Benedict, Tommy on the Beach; Mike Gillies, ETE; Julia Graddy, Maupin House Publishing; Martin Kanigsberg, Belvedere House; Paul Kenson, Kenson Associates; John Krol, "Don't Say Sandwich To Me"; Winston Lippert, Richard Plumer Design; Christopher Love, CLDA, Inc; Leslie Mayberry, Atlantic Shores Resort; Michele Micka, The New World Symphony; Gary Miner, Group M; Stephen Nevitt, Stephen Nevitt Florist; Marvin Page, Claire Restaurant; J.P. Pelletier–Troupet, La Vitrine; Beatrice Pila, Puente + Pila; Thomas E. Pope, Architect; Jack Richards, Gertrude's; Denis Russ, Miami Beach Development Corp.; Israel Sands, Flowers & Flowers; Barry Slack, Slack, Rodriguez, Hulce; Howard Snoweiss, Joyce/Snoweiss Design; Raul Sotolongo, Cano, Sotolongo & Assoc.; William Spear, Spear Communities; Bret Taylor, South Beach Realty; Wade Whynot, GW; William Wagenaar, William Wagenaar Studio; Lynn Wilson, Lynn Wilson Associates; Jacqulyn Yde, Interior Designer.

Jerrod New, a staff designer at McGarry & Madsen, meticulously proofed the text and coordinated final production details.

Also, special thanks to Wendy Lochner, Senior Editor for Architecture at Van Nostrand Reinhold, and her assistant, Kelly Francis. They alternately encouraged and pushed us through the difficult phases of creating our first full–color book.

CONTENTS

Part 3: Creating A Dynamic Personal Style

Part 4: Resources and Index

INTRODUCTION

When I examine myself and my methods of thought, I come close to the conclusion that the gift of fantasy has meant more to me than my talent for absorbing positive knowledge.
-Albert Einstein

Rendering is the process of creating an illusion, a fantasy, brought to life by the visual powers of your imagination. When you draw a rendering of a design, you are an illusionist—a magician, of sorts. And, like a magician, your act is based on a lot of carefully practiced skills; most of which, if executed well, your audience doesn't even notice.

But, unlike a magician, it helps tremendously if you believe the illusions as you develop them. Once you carry your imagination through the paper which is your picture plane, and play and enjoy the illusions on the other side, your efforts will rise confidently above the commonplace.

Our goals in this book are to teach you the skills of creating a three–dimensional illusion on a two–dimensional paper surface using color markers, along with a few sleight–of–hand "tricks" of the rendering trade, and to help you both enjoy and participate in the magic.

We use a question–and–answer format to make the material more accessible and direct. Each of the 40 questions frames a mini–lesson that you can master individually.

A total of 65 different tricks, simplified techniques, and tips are also highlighted throughout the text. Don't be embarrassed to use any or all of them. They are not gimmicks. Each one is supported by sound principles of art and design .

However, this book does not focus on principles, concepts, and theory. It's about ready–to–use solutions to a basic, everyday problem that all designers face: pulling together a fast, effective presentation rendering on short notice. The following pages provide new techniques and resources for using color markers, mixed with other media, that will give your design presentations the extra impact necessary to sell your concepts in today's competitive marketplace.

Part 1: Marker Rendering Basics

What are the advantages of using ink line and color markers for design presentations?

Markers possess a combination of qualities that make them an ideal rendering tool for busy designers. They require no set–up or clean–up time like watercolor and gouache, and are always ready–to–go; just uncap and start drawing.

Their consistent, predictable colors also mean that once you establish a sequence of markers that works to render the form of a particular subject—such as oak paneling or grass, for example—you can recreate the same effect again and again in future pictures. A success in one picture, if you stop and take a few color notes from the barrels of your pens, means you don't have to reinvent a solution each time you're confronted with a similar problem. So your work goes faster.

Markers are filled with bright, transparent dye color, usually in a solvent vehicle of alcohol or xylol. Unlike most paints, which depend on finely ground particles of pigment and an adhesive compound to bind them to the paper, marker dyes are simply floated into the paper surface by the solvent and absorbed. This allows the repeated application of several layers of color before any bleeding or muddiness occurs.

Ink line makes an appropriate complement to marker color because it assists in overcoming one of marker's major weaknesses: an inability to define and hold crisp edges. Disposable, water-based pens (such as the *Pilot RazorPoint* and *Sanford Breeze*) are not dispersed by the solvents in the popular marker brands, so they enable you to build a crisp base drawing to add color to.

Colored pencils are another medium used to complement marker renderings. They are usually added as a finishing touch, to modulate the color and texture over an area of marker color, providing a counterpoint to the flat, smooth marker color.

Markers are an ideal medium for rapid visualization and concept sketches. Subtlety is not a strong point, however; they require a direct, bold approach to be effective.

Another limitation of markers is that they don't mix as easily as water-based paint media. You have to overlay a series of colors to approximate the look of light, highlight, shade and shadow. Discovering the right color overlay combination can be a time-consuming process, but this book provides sets ready-to-go for everyday situations in the pages ahead.

Try it!

A standard blunt-tip marker has three working surfaces that provide a medium, thick, and extra-thick line width. However, if you use varying positions between these surfaces, and fluctuate your pressure on the marker and how fast you move it across the page, dozens of different calligraphic marks are possible. Try making an abstract composition using one blunt-tip marker in a calligraphic manner. Make as many different, interesting marks as you can. Limit each set of marks to a 4" x 6" area, and use a black marker. Be bold and dramatic.

3

Which manufacturer's line of color markers is best?

That depends on whom you ask. Every professional illustrator has a favorite brand; but most pick and choose from other manufacturers' lines to augment their color palettes.

Each of the major brands has a special feature that makes it right for certain situations. The double–ended *Berol Prismacolor* markers offer the convenience and economy of "two markers in one." *Chartpak AD* features a large color line and easily interchangable tips, while *Pantone* offers an even larger color selection, and its colors coordinate with the *Pantone Color Matching System.* Eberhard Faber now offers both its *Design Art* markers, with a xylene base, and the new *Design 2* line, which is alcohol–based, and has abolished the traditional cute names in favor of a color–wheel based nomenclature.

The fumes from the solvent xylene, used in some marker lines, can cause headaches if not used in a well–ventilated room.

There wasn't always such a profusion of choices. When first introduced in the 1960s, markers were constructed as little glass jars with a felt tip secured to a screw–on lid, under the brand name *Magic Markers.* Although awkward to hold and prone to color variations from batch to batch, those early markers revolutionized the world of architectural and advertising art.

They didn't require the set–up and clean–up time of traditional paint media. Colors dried in seconds after application, meaning layers of tints could be applied

rapidly. Plus, the dye colors had a radiant, watercolor quality.

Over the following decades the little glass bottles became ubiquitous in design offices around the world. An onslaught of more sophisticated brands of markers, with easier–to–hold barrels and palettes of several hundred colors, eventually drove *Magic Markers* off the market.

Markers are still evolving as an artist's tool, with new color and features issued regularly. If you are purchasing a set of markers for the first time, take time to evaluate the virtues and drawbacks of different brands. Does the shape of the barrel feel comfortable? Would you rather have a choice of several different points on separate markers, or a multi-purpose double–ended marker? Are you attracted to the logic of a color range laid out in carefully spaced values at specific points of the color wheel, or do you prefer a collection created and named for specific uses, such as wood tones, foliage, brick, or metals?

Once you invest all the time required to become comfortable using one line of markers, it's hard to switch. Your time is the biggest investment you will make.

Another tip: only select from leading brands that have been around for a while, are readily available in your area, and come in a range of at least 100 colors. Anything less is not adequate for professional design presentation needs.

Also, bear in mind that, if your presentation drawings will be on display for more than a few weeks, markers may not be the appropriate medium. Certain colors, such as the lavenders and purples, will fade noticeably with just a few days of continuous exposure to light. Others take several months to begin softening, but all marker dye colors fade. Since the purpose of most renderings is communication of a design concept rather than artistic expression, and most renderings have a useful life span of only a few days before being relegated to a file drawer anyway, this may be a shortcoming you can overlook.

Keeping your marker renderings and sketches stored in a dark place (such as a file drawer or rolled in a tube) will extend their life virtually indefinitely. If you must display them for more than a few days, try to keep your drawing away from bright spotlights or direct sun. A glass or plastic cover that contains ultraviolet screening additives will slow the fading process slightly.

When you do want an enduring record of a marker rendering, a 35mm slide is a simple, effective way to achieve it. For more information on photographing your renderings, see Question #40.

Try it!

Don't throw away old markers when they start to fade and streak. They are still useful in two different ways.

First, the streaky quality of a partially dried marker is great for textures, such as wood grain, grass cloth wall-covering, and rough stucco. Also, most old markers can be revived and used again with just the addition of some fresh solvent. Dried out markers often still have plenty of pigment in them, but not enough liquid left to let it flow out onto your paper.

All you need to do to revive your old markers is pull the tip out, and add a few drops of the appropriate solvent with an eye dropper, then reinsert the tip. For alcohol based markers, such as Prismacolor Art Markers, buy 91% alcohol solution at the drugstore; for other markers, use lighter fluid.

Your revived marker will be lighter in value and color intensity than a new marker—but that can be an asset when you're looking for an especially pale shade to work with.

Markers can easily imitate the bright, clear style of a watercolor. *Medium: markers on plastic-coated diazo paper; Illustrator: Barbara Ratner; Designer: Cooper Carry & Assoc.; Project: Barnett Bank, Jacksonville, FL.*

BUILDING 400 - PHASE I

BUILDING 400 - PHASE I & II

"I believe that rendering what you think you see is more effective than carefully drawing exactly what's there," says Dan Harmon. "If you squint at things or you watch T.V. and 'freeze-frame' a scene in your mind, sometimes the images remind you of a watercolor, with lots of light edges and little spots of light glistening. I try to capture that in my pictures, with plenty of highlights that are almost pure white. It's a kind of 'impressionism.'"

Dan is based in Atlanta, and has illustrated a number of well-known projects over the years, including many John Portman designs. He begins a rendering by developing the perspective on tracing paper, then transferring the drawing to *Strathmore High-Profile* illustration board, preferring the way it absorbs color compared to other surfaces. "Markers don't seem to bleed across it, but, at the same time, color soaks into the paper and doesn't sit on the surface like with coated papers."

He then begins working with a #2 pencil, adding foliage, people, and other compositional elements, erasing and revising. "Illustrations need to be designed around a focal point. There should be a hierarchy of visual information, where the most important feature is emphasized and then your eyes move to the less important parts, then finally the details.

White surfaces can be difficult to draw until you recognize the range of cool and warm grays needed to portray light falling across them. In this illustration Dan gives a virtuoso demonstration of how to handle an all-white interior. *Medium: markers on illustration board; Designer: John Portman & Associates, Atlanta, GA; Project: Shanghai Centre*

"I arrange the entourage to accomplish this. Then I add some surprises—so that, when you look at the picture a second time, you find something new and unexpected."

When he starts painting with color markers, Dan concentrates on light/dark relationships, placing light shapes in front of dark, and vice-versa. The changes in value and color totally define the edges of forms, since Dan uses no line work in his renderings, but defining edges is never a problem. "My edge control is not all that precise when you really look at it closely. It's more like 'controlled chaos.' I've found that whatever you do in a rendering, as long there is a consistency—a line is consistently wide, or straight, or sloppy, for example—then everything will look fine."

Planning the direction of your marker strokes to run along vertical, horizontal, or vanishing perspective lines in you rendering will help to separate and define the various planes in your picture. Here, Dan Harmon also uses secondary diagonal strokes to add reflected light effects and occasional vertical strokes over horizontal surfaces imply reflections. *Medium: markers on illustration board; Designer: John Portman & Associates; Project: Embarcadero Center West.*

How do different papers affect the working qualities of markers?

The two properties of paper most prized by designers and illustrators are transparency and ability to saturate with color dye. Unfortunately, they are inversely related: the more transparent a paper is, the less color absorption possible, and vice versa.

Most marker renderings are done on layout paper, which falls somewhere in between these two properties. It is reasonably translucent and allows some color saturation.

Tracing papers, such as drafting vellum and "bumwad" sketch rolls, are more transparent but absorb little color, leaving most of the dye simply sitting on the paper surface. They have a secondary advantage that, since the color is never fully absorbed into the paper fibers, most colors are erasable once dry.

At the other extreme are specially prepared "marker papers," which are preferred by art directors for ad comps but not often used for architectural illustration. They accept color beautifully and evenly, but are difficult to trace through.

Illustration board and colored mat board are also used by some artists who prefer their sturdy, reworkable surface, which does not buckle under paint or repeated erasures. The main drawback of illustration board is that any preliminary studies must be transferred to the board with graphite paper.

Although marker manufacturers pro-

The absorbent quality of the illustration board used for this rendering makes it possible to build rich, saturated colors and hold a crisp edge. *Medium: marker on illustration board; Illustrator: Dan Harmon; Designer: John Portman and Associates; Project: Marquis II Office Tower.*

vide color charts for their products, marker colors vary radically between papers with different absorption levels, so it's invaluable to make your own color charts on the specific papers you intend to use. To fully explore the possibilities of each marker in your chart, show what both one and two layers of color look like, since most papers accept a second layer without disturbing the first one.

Architect's sketch paper has a low absorbency ability, but is an easy surface for erasures and corrections. Color can also be applied to both side of the the paper. *Medium: ink and markers on sketch vellum; Designer and Illustrator: Ace Torre, Design Consortium, Ltd.; Project: Memphis Zoo, Memphis, TN.*

Shortcut

If you prefer to do your finished rendering on illustration board, or any opaque surface where it's not possible to trace from your preliminary layout, try doing your layout in pencil on vellum, then sticking a sheet of masking frisket over your drawing when completed. Rub it briskly, then remove. Some of the pencil graphite adheres to to the frisket and, when you lay the frisket adhesive surface over your illustration board and rub lightly, it will transfer a pale version of your drawing onto the surface. This saves you the laborious process of transferring the layout by tracing onto the board with graphite transfer paper.

What other media can I use to enhance my marker renderings?

"An artist must be ruthless. Do whatever you have to do to get the image you want," was the credo of Henry Carmean, a popular instructor at Art Center College for many years. His attitude is echoed by professional illustrators like Richard Radke of the Radke-Voss studio: "We use just about everything. In fact, if you saw a drawing table while one of our illustrators is in the midst of a project, it's covered with markers, *Pentels*, paint, ball-point pens, pastels—whatever it takes."

Markers alone are not an all-purpose medium. They are ideal for laying down large areas of bright, flat color quickly but are not as effective as other media for creating textures and color gradations, or overlaying opaque color.

Many illustrators start by blocking in color areas with markers, using their color brightness and consistency to advantage, then turn to colored pencils for subtle color "flavorings" and gradations. Colored pencil is also the tool of choice for highlights and sharpening the edges of color areas.

A white pencil is usually used for highlights, but there are other alternatives for special situations. Silver pencil often reads better against a dark background, or a very light tint of the area color for an atmospheric effect. Also, a cool color, such as a pale blue or lilac can be used along the edge of a dark object to create a halo backlit effect and to define the shape more clearly.

Colored pencils used with a blunt point or the side of the point are also good for textures. Smooth vellum papers can only accept a light layer of colored pencils, so start with a paper with a visible tooth when building layers of pencil color.

When using a colored pencil for thin, opaque lines, twirl the pencil as you pull it along a straight edge to keep the point longer. An electric pencil sharpener is a must for speedy execution.

Colored pencils are great for adding small details on top of color marker areas. It's also possible to reapply a light wash of marker over the colored pencil details to soften them; however, if applied too heavily, the solvent in the markers will melt the colored pencil details and

Try it!

"If you use blueline or other diazo papers just the way they are, marker color tends to spread as it's applied, creating a fuzzy edge," says illustrator Richard Radke. "The way I overcome this problem is to close the tooth of the paper by shaving pastel onto it. First, you scrape the edge of a hard pastel stick, such as *NuPastel* in white or cream, directly onto the rendering surface with a knife or single-edge razor blade, until a pile of powder has accumulated on the paper. Then rub it in with a tissue until the powder is completely absorbed by the paper. Any excess pastel can be dusted off."

One of the great benefits of this technique is that it can also be used to create special effects. For example, if you want to subtly highlight the center of the rendering, use white pastel there, then fade into gray pastel shavings at the edge of the picture. This helps to strengthen the focal point, even before applying any markers!

"I also use pastel shavings to color–key the rendering to a warm or cool scheme, or to lay down a base color for difficult surfaces," adds Richard. "Try blending in a tint of pastel over the entire surface of your rendering to subtly change the whole picture. The same markers look different on differently tinted papers, so you can use the identical markers—but get different effects—using paper prepared with pastel tints. For example, red pastel can be the base color for an expanse of red marble in a rendering, so that you only need to use beige and gray markers to tint and vein it." An area to be deeply tinted may have to be masked using a low–tack drafting tape first, however.

Illustrator Bob McAllen proves that even the most unlikely combinations of media can prove effective with this mix of markers, colored inks, and gouache, applied to colored mat board. *Designers: Bob McAllen and Tom McClure; Project: "Venice Street Scene" for theme park concept.*

clog the marker tip with pencil sediment.

Gouache (the most popular brand is *Winsor & Newton Designers Gouache*) is great for opaque color overlay, especially fine lines of light over a dark background. The marker color will tend to bleed through slightly with some colors, especially where the gouache overlay is very light, so it should be used in the thickest consistency possible. Large areas of gouache will buckle unmounted papers; it is usually reserved for small spots and lines of intense color.

Pastel sticks can be used to make smoothly gradated, atmospheric backgrounds with soft edges by scraping a pastel stick to get granulated particles, which you can apply with a ball of cotton. The soft color effect can then be worked over with markers. Pastels can even be used to approximate an airbrush effect in many situations.

Trick

It can be especially difficult to take risks and be confident when confronted with a blank, white sheet of paper, and the expectation that a brilliant, polished rendering will somehow arise from it. Tell yourself that you're doing just another preliminary study overlay and not the final drawing—even though it is. The 19th–century philosopher William James called this "the willing suspension of disbelief." Then admit to yourself that it's the final draft once the drawing is underway and going well.

Bob McAllen

When Bob McAllen starts a sketch rendering, his first decision is what color of mat board to use. But instead of using it to frame the finished picture, he draws on the colored board. "It becomes an instant color scheme for the rendering, and unifies the picture from the very beginning, so I don't need to add as much marker color," says Bob.

Using markers, colored inks, and gouache accents on mat board is the fastest technique he knows of. "I use this technique when there's almost no time to do anything at all. When I need to do eight or ten sketches a week, the kind that make a strong impression without getting into detail, this is how I do it."

After receiving approval on a preliminary thumbnail sketch, he lays out the drawing in pencil directly on the board, skipping the tedious work of developing the drawing on vellum and then transferring it to a board. "I try to do all my preliminary drawing right on the board. If I run into any problems in the drawing, I abandon it and start again on a new board," he adds.

The double–ended *Berol Prismacolor* markers are currently Bob's favorite brand. He applies the marker color over his drawing, adds some areas of airbrush ink dyes for atmosphere, and finishes up with white and light tints of gouache for accents. "It's a lot easier to add the highlighted areas when you're finished than it is to leave the white areas untouched and carefully work around them, as you would in working on a regular white board."

The beige color of the board helps the artist create the illusion of glowing lights. It creates an overall background tone that makes the white highlights "pop." Medium: Marker, airbrushed ink dyes, and gouache on colored mat board; Designer: R. Duell & Associates; Project: Casino and Gaming Room.

Simple color schemes have the potential for dramatic results. "Here I've got a blue–green sky, which is almost a direct complement on the color wheel to the board color, some drawing, a few white highlights, and that's about all there is," explained Bob. *Medium: Marker, airbrushed ink dyes, and gouache on colored mat board; Designer: V. Nelhiebel & W. Pierce; Project: Urban Design Study*

Try to visualize this composition without the sailboat to understand the impact a single piece of entourage can have on a rendering. *Medium: Marker, airbrushed ink dyes, and gouache on colored mat board; Designer: Bob McAllen; Project: Floating Restaurant Concept.*

It's hard for me to lay down an even area of color in markers. What should I do?

First of all, don't drive yourself crazy trying for absolutely perfect, flat areas of color. It is a difficult goal to achieve and usually not worth the effort. What is most often needed are simply areas of color that are not overly streaky; little variations in color actually add vitality to a picture and should be saved whenever possible.

Try to lay down large areas of color in a series of brisk sweeps with a blunt tip marker, picking up the wet leading edge of the previous stroke with the top of the next stroke. The leading edge of color should be reswept with a fresh stroke of color fast enough so that it doesn't have a chance to dry until the entire strip is filled with color.

The adhesive edge of sheets of *Post-It* message pads can be used to make a quick, simple mask for short straight edges when laying down a marker wash.

If you slow down the speed of your stroke at the end of a sweep in order to stop exactly at an edge, more color will be absorbed into the paper at the end of the strokes; so keep the speed of your arm movement as consistent as possible.

When applying markers with a straight edge, lift the edge off the paper slightly to avoid color bleed under the edge. This is not necessary if you are using a thick, beveled edge.

Where a complicated shape must be filled in, try using a masking tape or frisket for edge control. Ordinary low-tack drafting tape works fine on most papers, but should not be left in

position for more than a few hours because the adhesive bond increases over time, eventually causing paper tears when removed.

When using papers with low absorbency, like drafting vellum, masking is not necessary for edge control. You can sweep the strokes of color past the edges of your shape, then use a clear "blender" marker to refloat and absorb color beyond the edges later. An electric eraser will also lift off most marker color on drafting vellum and film.

When even color flow is critical, use a "juicy" new marker. As a marker gets used up, the uneven ink flow makes flat color washes impossible. Older markers are fine for smaller color areas, however, and partially dried-out ones are perfect for creating textures.

To make a soft area of color with graduated tones, apply solvent (such as lighter fluid or alcohol) to the area with a cotton pad—or cotton swab for small areas—then float color into it while still moist. More solvent can be applied with a cotton pad to further blend colors after the first wash has dried.

Airbrush attachments for markers are another way to get an even tone, with soft, feathered edges as a bonus. Both *Pantone* and *Design Art* have attachments for their markers that send a thin stream of compressed air over the tip to approximate an airbrush effect. Always start the flow of ink by testing the spray on a scrap piece of paper before using it on your rendering; it often takes a while to get the dye flowing properly.

Whenever possible, modulate your surfaces to keep them interesting. Avoid flat, even areas of tone. A simple way to modulate the color on a surface is to fill in the color from the front edge to the back (or vice–versa) and double–back over the last few strokes.

Usually, the modulation of color is done by lightening the front edge and darkening the receding edge of an object. But compositional factors can cause you to reverse this.

Work from light to dark when applying markers because, as with any transparent color medium, light color can always be made darker, but not the other way around.

Shortcut

When you are applying color to a diazo or xerographic print, an easy way to cut a paper frisket for masking background areas for airbrush (or the special "airbrush" attachments for markers) is to make several extra prints of the base drawing on lightweight paper. Then cut each mask out of a lightweight paper copy and align it over your rendering.

Make your "frisket copies" on oversize sheets of paper, if possible, to give yourself extra protection around the perimeter of the rendering for overspray.

No attempt is made to conceal the marker strokes in this sketch; instead, they contribute to the spontaneous feel of the drawing. *Medium: marker and colored pencil on a blackline diazo print of drawing; Illustrator and Designer: Michael Borne, AIA, Selzer Associates, Inc.; Project: Esplanade Mall, Baton Rouge, LA.*

The lighting looks drab in my renderings. How do I make it bright and crisp?

Every professional illustrator interviewed for this book was asked the following question: "What do you consider to be the most important element for making a dramatic rendering?" All but two said that "light" is their #1 dramatic tool. The other two considered "contrast" the most important dramatic element, but then went on to explain that it is primarily achieved through dramatic lighting.

To a pro, light *is* rendering. It creates the viewer's understanding of the forms depicted, generates the value contrasts necessary to separate the forms from each other, and adds sparkle to the picture.

Yet light itself cannot be drawn; only its effects. Conscientiously studying the way light falls across the forms you see every day is how you improve your drawing of its effects.

Actually "seeing" light effects requires a change in the way you see things. Ordinarily you look at objects for the useful information that light gives you about their shape, texture, and color.

Even though a yellow box, for example, may have a strip of white highlight gleaming along a top edge, a muddy ocher color on the side that's in shade, perhaps a reflection of a pink background blended into its glossy top surface, and a deep gray shadow that it casts on the white surface it's sitting on, your mind sees only the yellow color that it shows in direct, frontal light and uses the rest of the colors to interpret the box's shape, finish, and how it sits in its surroundings. In effect, your brain acts in a computer-like fashion to process all those colors into information you can use to reach out and pick up the object or, perhaps, walk around it.

Rendering involves learning *not* to process the raw visual data in front of your eyes, but simply to observe the colors and shapes as they are. It will require intense concentration at first to make the shift in your consciousness necessary to see things simply "as they are."

Here are some things to look for when observing light effects:

With single-source light, every different surface of an object is a different value (shade of gray) because it reflects a different amount of light to your eyes.

The edges of shadows soften as they move away from their casting source. Shadows cast by tall, thin objects, such as street-light poles, fade rapidly as they move away from the pole—due to atmospheric fill light.

Shade and shadow areas are often darker than they may first appear.

The edges of large shadow areas often appear darker than the inside.

In real life, an object can contain dozens of different values over its surface. But renderers often simplify it to four: light, highlight, shade, and shadow.

Try it!

To better understand the dramatic effects that light creates, try cutting out little pieces of magazine photos and laying them on a white sheet of paper to observe. Look at photos of objects that are all one color. Then cut out a tiny piece of the shadow area, shade, light, and highlight, and lay them apart on a white paper. Notice how they look very different standing alone, out of the context of the picture.

As an alternative, cut a 1/4" square hole in a piece of heavy white paper, hold it about 12" in front of you, close one eye, and look through it at the light, highlight, shade, and shadow areas of an object, comparing them to the white paper surface that frames the hole.

"Light" is defined as the area that receives full, direct light. "Highlight" is the limited area that directly reflects light back at the viewer. "Shade" is the area that does not receive direct light, but does get reflected light bounced onto it from adjacent surfaces. "Shadow" is the absence of light on a surface caused by another object blocking the light from reaching it (casting a shadow). Shadows often do not receive reflected, "fill" light, and are darker than shade.

Since most marker sets come with a 10-value gray set, it is easiest to explain light based on a 10-step gray system. The simplified value sequences shown below are set up with the top surface of the box as the highlight value, left surface as the light value, right surface as shade, and a cast shadow on the ground plane.

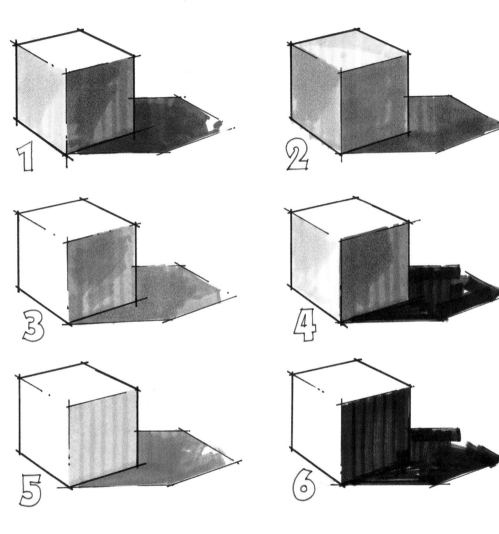

Box 1 has a straightforward, standard value spectrum (White, Gray #3, Gray #8, and Gray #9), while box 2 is a more diffused, soft lighting (Gray #2, Gray #5, Gray #7, Gray #8). A simplified system is used for box #3, with one value for both light and highlight, and a second one for shade and shadow (White, White, Gray #7, Gray #7). Box 4 emphasizes the shadow value with black (White, Gray #2, Gray #8, Black), as opposed to the high-key values of Box 5 (White, White, Gray #5, Gray #7). The highly stylized values of Block 6 are dramatic but have limited uses (White, White, Black, Black).

More pointers on using light:

▨ Don't be afraid to use bright light and strong, dark shadows. People are psychologically attracted to light and repelled by darkness. Rich, radiant light is inviting, while darkness is ominous, scary; overcast light is dreary and depressing for most people.

▨ Establish the darkest dark and the lightest light right at the start of adding the colors and values to a rendering in order to give a range to judge the rest of the values against.

▨ Shadows define the shapes they fall across. Let long shadows stream across your picture, running up and over objects in their path.

▨ Use a minimum of four values for a highly rendered object: light, highlight, shade, and shadow. For simplified work, use three values: light, shade, and shadow. For background or low-key illustration, try two values: light and one value for both shade and shadow combined.

Trick!

To get a lighter tint of a marker color, touch the nib on a solvent-soaked pad or wad of cotton or a small cup of alcohol before applying the color. This lightens the color for the next few strokes only. It's an especially effective way of doing highlights when a very light value of the color you need is not available.

░ Shadows are rarely black and can actually be lighter than the shade side of a very dark object casting the shadow.

░ Darken the edges of large shadows to create more contrast.

░ Remember that reflected light picks up the color of the reflecting surface and projects it onto adjacent surfaces.

░ Play with patterns of light and dark, as you subdivide your picture into large areas. Set up your values in preliminary study (like the one at left).

░ Portray objects in shadow as carefully as those in direct light, but in a lower key, with closer values. Fill light will cast shadows in the same direction as direct light, but in a softer, darker manner.

░ Vary the light across each surface of your rendering, fading values slightly from one edge to the other. Notice how the burglar alarm console box, below, has modulated values over each side.

░ Whenever possible, plan ahead to leave the white of your paper as the highlight value.

Low-gloss surfaces require a subtle reflection and mild highlights. *Medium: marker and white gouache on* Canson Pro-Layout *marker paper; Illustrator: the authors; Project: Burglar alarm console box for Seaboard Systems, Inc.*

How can I best indicate people in my sketch renderings?

Adding people to architectural renderings often presents a dilemma for designers: although they are necessary to show the scale and usage of a building, a cluster of beautifully rendered people can easily steal the show and obscure the real focus of your picture: the design. People are only another kind of entourage—that sets up an environmental stage to show off your concepts. And, although thoughtfully arranged figures add life to a rendering, poorly drawn or placed people only confuse and clutter up a picture.

Human figures that work within the context of a rendering should harmonize with the style and level of detail of the rest of the picture. Sometimes realistic, carefully–drawn people are necessary for a highly detailed, refined rendering, and they are discussed further in Question #35. But what is most often required for design sketches is called an "indication": a loose, casual drawing with a low level of detail, often highly stylized.

The stylized approach is easiest and, if you take the time to memorize a few of the basic shapes necessary, they can be executed quite rapidly. We have demonstrated a few at left, and named them for their endearing, eccentric qualities.

An investment of a few hours' practice to memorize their outlines will enable you to develop a kind of rubber stamp kit that you carry around in your head, ready at a second's notice for a series of quick imprints on your drawing.

Gesture rates more important than accuracy when doing a stylized figure indication. The figures also don't need to be strongly dimensional; a graphic, cut–out look is appropriate. But they must look animated and be drawn in a confident, relaxed style.

Where a cluster of people is indicated, you can often delete most of the detail except the outline surrounding the cluster. Also, an odd number of people, such as 3 or 5, seems to look better than an even number for some inexplicable reason. A single person gives most pictures a decidedly lonely feeling; people look better grouped and interacting with each other.

When a higher level of detail and realism is required, then the basic proportions, dimensions, and shapes of human anatomy need to be learned. The most important element of anatomy for the architectural artist is not a specific body part, but the proportional relationships between them.

The human head is most often used as a convenient measuring unit for establishing body proportions. It's an effective device because the head is the single part of the body most often scaled out of proportion by beginners. The head gets an inordinate amount of attention whenever

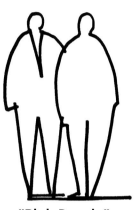

"Blob People"

"Floating Head People"

"Square Heads That Always Have Their Hands In Their Pockets"

observing a person, and the eyes, mouth, and facial shapes are how we remember people. Tremendous significance is attached to their gestures; but that doesn't make it okay to draw the head grossly over–scale, as often happens in first attempts to render the human figure.

The average human is 7 ½ heads high. However, most illustrators render it at 8 heads high for convenience and to create more appealing proportions. Fashion illustrators often push the limit out to 9 heads high, generating a very leggy, ideal figure. Michelangelo stretched the ratio to 10, and sometimes 11, heads for his epic sculptures and paintings.

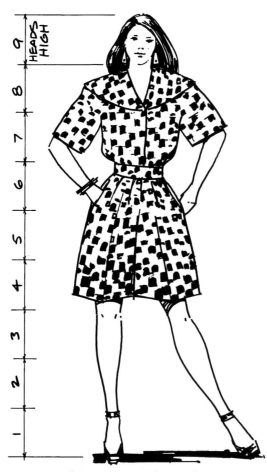

"Fashion Proportion" Figure

But 8 heads is the best proportion to work with for most situations because it subdivides easily to create reference points for developing a figure. To block in a human figure from scratch, draw a line the height of the figure you need to sketch, and mark the top and bottom with a short notch. Then subdivide the length into two equal parts, and subdivide those parts again to effectively divide

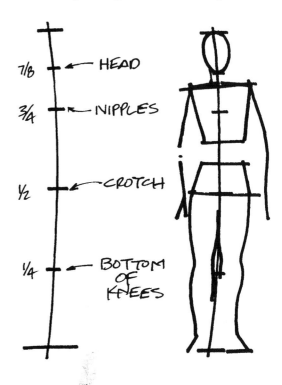

the length in quarters. The midpoint of the figure is at the level of the genitals, and the quarter points fall at the nipples and bottom of the kneecaps. Subdivide the top quarter again, and you have marked off the height of the head, equal to one eighth of a person's overall height.

Next, loosely draw in a square for the chest (rib cage mass), a second rectangle of equal width, but half the height, to create the hip part of the torso. Leave a gap between the two, where the waist line falls, then taper both both slightly towards the waist.

These two shapes, the chest and hips, connect through the spine and rarely align exactly in real life. When a standing person puts more weight on one leg than the other—which is usually the case—the hip mass is tilted up on the weight bear-

Technique

People are always easiest to draw in simple front, back, or side views, where they can be constructed as a graphic shape, without complicated perspective considerations. When you're in a hurry, avoid 3/4 or angled views.

ing side and chest mass is tiled down toward the weight bearing side.

The same tilt occurs towards the weight–bearing leg when walking. Also, people walking briskly counterbalance their leg movement with an opposite movement of their arms. In other words, when the left leg is forward, the left arm is back, and vice–versa.

The basic shapes are adjusted slightly to differentiate between men and women. The male figure has a larger chest and smaller hips, drawn in a more angular style, whereas the female is more rounded, with larger hips and a smaller chest.

To draw children, reduce the number of heads in height according to age. A 3–year–old is 5 heads high, with a wide, round face, narrow shoulders and virtually no neck. The center of the body is at the belly button, which creates a long torso in proportion to the legs. As a child grows older, the antomical center of the body gradually shifts down towards the genitals, and the head grows smaller in proportion to the rest of the body: 6 heads at age 6, 6½ heads at age 8, and 7 heads at puberty. The neck and shoulders also grow with age, and the face becomes longer and less rounded.

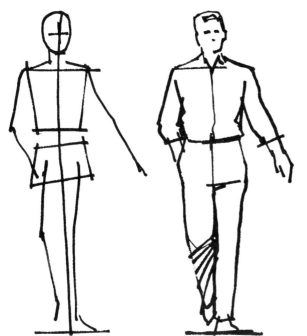

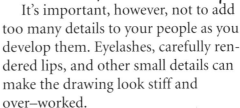

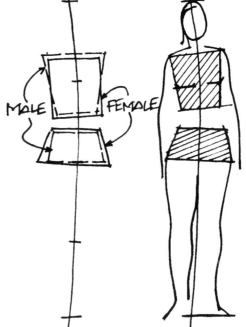

Most professional illustrators include people in their compositions right from the start. "I put people in from the very beginning of my sketches," says Eric Hyne. "They start out as big blobs with a dot at the top for a head, done with a fat marker. Then, as the drawing develops, the people develop too. I develop the trees, the people, and architecture together as the picture progresses. It's a process of gradually bringing them into focus, and developing detail. All three elements are part of my overall composition."

For side and three-quarter views of people, apply the same proportions but be sure to show the curvature of the spine and the fact that the neck angles forward from the torso (not straight up!).

It's important, however, not to add too many details to your people as you develop them. Eyelashes, carefully rendered lips, and other small details can make the drawing look stiff and over–worked.

So relax! Don't agonize over your people. Instead try to create a flowing line and a gesture or movement in each of the figures.

Try to keep within the boundaries of the basic proportions we have outlined for you, but don't be afraid to vary them a little as you feel necessary. As the 16th–century writer Francis Bacon observed, "There is no excellent beauty that hath not some strangeness in the proportion."

"I was a little girl that drew horses all the time," says Barbara Ratner. "Drawing three–dimensional objects always appealed to me. But, when I was going to architecture school, rendered images were just not popular. Every thing was plans and elevations, ink on *Mylar*."

Tip

To do a sketch rendering in a hurry, Barbara makes a washed–out blackline diazo print of a perspective block–out; then she develops her final color–marker rendering immediately, directly over it. "Make the print so overexposed that you can barely see your lines, and they act only as a reference for edges," she adds. "Work loosely, first using color markers exclusively, then finish up with some black or sepia line drawing to sharpen and define areas that have become mushy."

It wasn't until after college, on her first job, that she started volunteering for any office project that involved doing a rendering of the design and discovered she had a talent for it. Most of her later education in architectural illustration has been what she categorizes as 'on–the–job training' and a few seminars along the way."

Barbara works on plastic–coated diazo blackline paper, also known as clay–coat diazo. "It's great for blending colors. You can build up to as many as four or five layers of color, and it seems the more layers you put on, the better it gets. I've seen some renderings using this technique that look so much like watercolor that most people can't tell the difference. You get a very loose, watery look."

Sky color spills over into the building and foreground paving, creating a luminous effect and a unified color scheme. *Medium: markers on plastic-coated diazo paper; Designer: Carlson Assoicates Inc.; Project: Place Vendome.*

When the paper starts to feel gummy to the touch, you've reached the saturation point and it's time to stop," she adds. Barbara finishes up using a little gouache paint for details and to accent edges, but rarely adds colored pencil because it doesn't adhere well to her favorite coated paper stock.

For a change of pace, she recommends *AZON #1932*, a matte finish blackline diazo paper, which does accept colored pencil and pastel and holds a crisp edge of marker color but is not suitable for color blending techniques.

People can be both loosely rendered and realistic, as this illustration demonstrates. *Medium: markers on plastic-coated diazo paper; Designer: Turner & Associates; Project: Ben Hill Methodist Church.*

Very little of the foliage in this rendering is actually green, and most of the greens used are subdued; yet it has a rich, lush quality. *Medium: markers on plastic-coated diazo paper; Designer: Cooper Carry & Associates; Project: Rocky Gap.*

I always have trouble matching the colors I've selected for a rendering. What is the best way to copy color sample swatches?

If you spend all your energy trying to exactly match a color chip in a rendering, you will both frustrate yourself and end up with a boring rendering too. That's because rendering is about the effect of light falling over the various surfaces of an object in three dimensions, and each surface reflects light differently.

Both the color and the intensity of light also vary over larger flat surfaces. Even when an object is entirely one color, each surface on it will appear to be a different tint and intensity of the color because of the way light is hitting it.

Often, only a single spot of color in a successful rendering of an object will approximately match the object's true color, but the rendition of light, highlight, shade, and shadow effects will give an overall impression of the correct color. To demonstrate this phenomenon for yourself, try holding a color chip under a bright, single light source and tilt it at different angles to observe how the color your eye perceives changes dramatically with the angle at which you tilt it.

So, how can you possibly hope to match a color chip if light effects cause perceived color to vary widely over the surface of an object? Relax: light effects actually work to your advantage. The best way to match a color is to "dance around it" on the color wheel, rather than attempting to precisely match it. If you introduce subtle variations in the color on every plane of the object you are rendering, your picture looks more lively and loose, and you don't have to struggle to pin down one "exactly correct" color.

There are several easy techniques for creating slight color variations with markers:

■ Before applying the color, put down a layer of a light version of its comple-

ment (the color directly opposite it across an artist's "color wheel") to subdue and nudge it towards gray. For example, start with a wash of light pink before applying green, or add some pale blue before applying orange.

Use a pale version of the color located on either side of it on the color wheel to create a slight variation in hue. Add a few strokes of pale green or pale purple before applying blue, for example.

A layer of cool or warm gray can also be applied before laying down your main color. However, this technique can create muddied, dirty–looking colors and should be used sparingly.

■ Adding a second layer of the same color will enrich the color intensity on the more absorbent papers, such as diazo print papers and some proprietary marker pads. With less–absorbent surfaces, all this does is smear the color around.

■ On translucent papers, like vellum, you can apply color on the back of the paper. It shows through only slightly, and is great for subtle gradations.

■ Color can also be subtly adjusted by changing the colors surrounding the one you are trying to match. This sophisticated technique is based on the principle that the colors around an object tend to tint the object with their complement on the color wheel in the viewer's perception. A green object surrounded by a red background (whose complement is green) will look richer than the same green object surrounded by a green background (whose complement is red), for example. And a green object surrounded by an orange background (whose complement is blue) will be perceived as slightly more blue–green.

■ A final layer of colored pencil varies color and adds texture. It's also effective

24

for smoothly gradated tones.

While it is only necessary to approximate a color in a rendering and then "dance around it" with light effects, color charts are still necessary to help you search for the nearest color to the one you are trying to portray. Most marker manufacturers provide printed color charts showing their entire line on a single sheet, but, since markers are dyes that depend on paper absorbency for their intensity, the actual color you get varies widely with different papers.

Most artists make their own color charts on sheets of the actual paper they most often use. Your color chart will be more useful to you if you apply a large square of each color, then add a couple of strokes of the the same color across one corner to show what two coats of it looks like. Then a stroke or two of modifying colors across the other three corners, with color notes and comments. Plastic page protectors with a three–ring punch are helpful if you intend to refer to your charts often and keep them in a notebook.

If the time–consuming task of making color charts of several hundred marker

Tip

"Two–handed" color mixing works great on less-absorbent papers like vellum: hold the dominant marker color you want to use in your drawing hand and a second, modifying color in the other hand. Dab a little of the modifying color on the rendering and immediately wipe over it with the main color. Continue applying color, adding a dab or streak of the modifying color just ahead of the strokes of the dominant color.

combinations is more than you want to endure, try the approach used by illustrator Michael Flynn. "I grab my project materials, go to the art supply store, and lay everything out on the floor in front of the marker display racks," according to Michael. "Then I go through all the markers—with fabric swatches and color chips in one hand, and a piece of the actual rendering paper I'm using in the other—and find the color matches and combinations I need."

When matching colors, remember that color is a quality, an effect, of light and can't be separated from it; always work under balanced light.

Medium: ink and markers on Bienfang Graphics #360 paper; Illustrator and Designer: Voytek Szczepanski.

Sometimes it seems like the more color I add to a drawing, the worse it gets. What am I doing wrong?

Only blue, beige, and gray markers were necessary to bring this sketch to life. *Medium: markers on xerographic reproduction drawing on bond paper; Illustrator: Sam Ringman; Designer: Neal Stewart / Design Associates, Inc.; Project: Crystal Store.*

Drawing engages the mind in a different mode of perception than painting. Both techniques use flat shapes to convey the illusion of three–dimensional form, and painting essentially builds on the foundation laid by a good drawing. But drawing defines shapes by outlining them, sometimes leaving the shape itself a void of white paper for the imagination to develop further; whereas painting portrays the area of the shapes themselves in a relationship closer to what is actually seen in life.

Drawing is a more abstract form of visual communication, since your mind's eye looks at the lines but actually comprehends the shapes enclosed. When you also render with paint or color markers all the shapes, values, and light effects inside the linework, the lines become superfluous. They seem to sit on top of the fully rendered areas, and the picture takes on the quality of a page from a child's coloring book.

Essentially, a rendering needs to fit into one of two categories: (1) it can be predominantly a drawing, with color added, like the office tower rendering at right, or (2) essentially a painting, with perhaps some linework to accentuate

the key shapes. When you completely finish a drawing so that it will stand alone without color, then add detailed color to the entire surface of the picture, perceptual problems occur. To avoid them, don't overcolor a drawn rendering or depend too heavily on line in one where the color and value of the markers themselves are strong enough to carry the picture.

Perhaps the simplest way to add color to a drawing is "color coding," by which you add flat areas of color to a few features of the rendering without modulating the color, in order to create the effect of light over the surfaces. It can only be done on a limited basis,

using two or three colors at most and leaving plenty of bare paper, but it does explain key colors and adds impact to a simple sketch rendering. If you are using three colors, try selecting a bright color to emphasize the most important part of the design, a second complementary color to highlight and frame the first one, and a third, muted color for a background wash. Keep it simple and don't be so splashy with the color that it overwhelms the drawing.

Another interesting technique is to add the accent colors on a dark diazo print—made by the running the drawing through the print machine significantly faster than usual. The low

Although this is a full-color rendering, the drawing defines most of the form. It is essentially an ink drawing with color added. Medium: watercolor and markers on a photomural paper reproduction of an ink drawing; Illustrator: the authors; Project: brochure announcing new offices for Chase Manhattan Private Bank.

Gray, used judiciously for contrast and to develop major shapes in a drawing, may be all that is necessary in some situations. *Medium: ink and gray makers on vellum; Illustrator and Designer: Syd Mead; Project: "LA 2015 Malibu Beach" concept.*

contrast creates a softer image and mutes the colors applied.

For more complex situations, you will need to show the effects of light on the surfaces and extend your palette to include more colors. But how do you keep your picture from turning into a circus of spots and stripes of color? First, limit and coordinate your color selections: try to reuse the same colors in several areas of the picture. The same light beige that is a highlight/reflection area on a walnut panel could possibly be reused as part of a carpet color; or, stray spots of colors used in your foliage can be dropped into the shadows of the architecture to add modulation.

Also, keep the overall picture either warm or cool and in one color key: for example, a cool picture with greens and blues predominating, or a warm picture with mostly pinks and beiges. This does not mean that you can't include other colors, but that one color should domi-nate the scheme to make a more unified picture.

When in doubt, use beige or gray instead of color. They are especially effective for making areas recede in a picture. Everything does not have to be rendered realistically and in full color.

If your line drawing is small enough to fit on the bed of your office photocopier, make several photocopies reduced to a convenient small size and use them to rapidly try out different color treatments. Even though the markers may not work as well on the copier paper, this system provides a quick set of "thumbnails" to experiment on.

Medium: color markers on
a blackline diazo print;
Illustrator: the authors;
Designer: Gail Byron
Baldwin, Architect; Project:
Duty Free Shop,
Fontainebleau Hilton
Resort, Miami Beach, FL.

Technique

Color can be used to visually "talk" about selected areas
in a design, by fully rendering the highlighted areas and
adding only spot color to the surrounding areas, as in
the renderings on this page. It's a great time-saver, too!

radke

When Richard Radke launched his career as an architectural illustrator thirty years ago, color markers came in a limited palette of only forty colors. "Color matching was a big problem, so we started mixing our own colors by unscrewing the felt tip, adding inks and dyes to the stock markers, then reinserting the tip. We still mix a lot of our own colors today, especially greens. There doesn't seem to be enough greens among the popular brands to suit our tastes; so, over the years, we have developed formulas for our own 'house' color variations."

His firm, Radke–Voss Collaborative, is a six–person team that divides up the phases of a rendering according to each artist's specialty. The layout is developed by one staff member, passed to another for entourage development, perhaps a third artist for drawing the people, and yet another for color application.

"We prefer *Chartpak AD* markers, mainly for their extensive color palette, but fill in some of the gaps in the *AD* line with *Design Art* markers," he adds. "For most renderings, we print the layout drawing on blueline paper, presentation weight, and mount it on heavy board with *Double Tack* (a brand of large sheets of double–stick adhesive paper, made by *Grafix*, available at art–supply stores). We roll our print out on the board, with the *Double Tack* in between. Since tempera is used for details and accents, the *Double Tack* keeps the print paper from buckling under the moisture of the paint. It's also available pre-laminated to a backup board, so all you have

Low-key reflections of the architecture in the foreground pavement are one of the liberties that professional illustrators often take to make a rendering more compelling. *Medium: marker, colored pencil and tempera on a blueline diazo print; Designer: Otis Associates, Architects; Project: Zurich Insurance Towers, Schaumburg, IL.*

Medium: marker, colored pencil, and tempera on a blueline diazo print; Designer: Wilson Jenkins & Associates, Inc.; Project: Novi Office Park, Novi, MI.

to do is roll out the layout print and bray it down with a roller."

The Radke–Voss Collaborative staff is always trying new color techniques, but, according to Richard, the preliminary steps in a rendering are always the most important. "We're sticklers about each perspective layout. It is the number one element for making a dramatic rendering. Always get the viewpoint, scale, and

details accurate before even thinking about color.

"For a more impressive perspective, I just get in closer," he adds. "Especially when doing an interior rendering, I always want it to feel as though the viewer is within the space, not taking a snapshot from a distance. It also helps to be close to a wall or piece of furniture in the foreground."

Medium: markers, colored pencil, and tempera on a blueline diazo print; Project: Deerbrook Mall, Deerbrook, TX.

Shortcut

When he needed to do two almost identical renderings on short notice a few years ago, Richard Radke scrambled to find a way to perform. "The interior materials were so important to the client for this stock–exchange rendering project," he explained, "that he wanted to see two renderings: first, only the room finishes, without people, and then another rendering full of activity. Unfortunately, there wasn't enough time in our schedule to do two renderings, so I proceeded to do a rendering without people, while my assistant simultaneously drew all the figures and foreground furniture on a copy of the layout. Then I finished the basic rendering and photographed it, while my assistant put a *Double Tack* backing on his version and carefully cut out all the entourage pieces. Finally, we applied them over my bare-bones rendering."

They met the deadline and in the process developed a technique that also makes it easier to fix errors or make design changes without redoing the rendering. You can patch in changes and additions using the same procedure. It's not necessary to cut out any parts of the changed area; just adhere the new section directly over it using *Double Tack*. The thickness of the paper is barely noticeable, even at an angle, because the Double Tack adheres evenly right up to the edge of the paper. "We have done major changes, like replacing an entire sky or taking out a few floors of a high–rise, using this patch method," Richard adds.

Medium: marker, colored pencil, and tempera on a blueline diazo print; Designer: Space Management Planning; Project: Board of Trade Trading Floor, Chicago, IL.

I tend to get bogged down in the details of laying out a perspective. How can I make it less confusing?

Accurate rendering is about proportion, not scale, and therein lies the secret of speeding up the layout of a rendering. Ideally, you should make only one scale measurement as the first step of a perspective construction, then everything that follows is proportional to that first arbitrary scale decision—on a sliding scale in space.

A tool called multiple dividers makes the many proportional calculations required in constructing a rendering easier. It is similar to a standard set of dividers, except that it has eleven points instead of two and, as it is expanded and contracted, the distance between each pair of points remains equal.

The technique for using multiple dividers hinges on one element that remains constant in a rendering: the height of the eye level (also called the horizon line). No matter where an object is located in the theoretical volume of a perspective construction, the eye level at that point remains a constant height above a reference ground plane (or below a reference ceiling plane). Although the distance between the floor and the eye level line, as measured on the surface of your drawing, varies according to where you are in the theoretical volume of the perspective, the designated distance between them—say five feet, for example—stays constant.

Multiple dividers, shown below, are also helpful for freehand preliminary studies, where overall proportion is important but exact detailing is not. You can quickly block in wall areas and furniture accurately, then refine the layout with drafting instruments in a series of overlays.

Photo: Ken Schiff

This means that you can pick any point of the floor plane of a rendering with a five–foot eye level, set the #0–point of the multiple dividers on it and the #5–point of the eye level directly above it, and the intermediate points mark off one–foot increments between them. Or, for smaller divisions, set the #10–point at the eye level for six–inch increments between intermediate points.

When constructing a tall object in a rendering with the five–foot eye level, set the #1–point at the eye level. This would generate a five–foot distance between points, meaning that a 30–foot height would fall at the #6–point. If the height you are trying to create is 28 feet, then mark off 25 feet and 30 feet at the #5– and #6–points, then reset the dividers between them to create five divisions, thereby locating the 28–foot height

between them accurately and easily.

Similarly, for a 3'–6" eye level, setting the #7–point on the eye level would result in 6" divisions between points and, for a 42–foot eye level, setting the #7–point on the eye level marks off six–foot divisions between points.

The system generates an instant "scale" measurement at any point in your rendering, and it can, of course, also be used for surfaces that are viewed in elevation.

Multiple dividers are not stocked in most art–supply stores, but they can be special–ordered.

Another way to speed up your renderings is called "multiplication of boxes." It's a perspective construction technique that begins with drawing a single, square box by eye and assigning it a dimension—like five feet, for example. Then, everything after that is constructed by multiplying you original box outward in whatever directions necessary to build a larger form.

Additional boxes are created by drawing a line from a corner of the first box through the midpoint of the opposite side, extending it until it crosses an extension of the bottom edge of the box. The midpoint of the side of the box can be found by drawing diagonals from the corners, then pulling a horizontal line over to the side from their intersection.

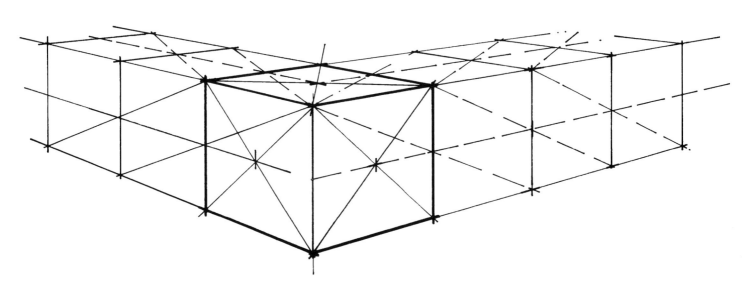

Boxes can also be subdivided in half, then halved again and again, using the intersection of diagonals.

Or, boxes can be subdivided by marking off divisions of the height of the box with multiple dividers, then projecting them over to a diagonal to the corners of the box, then pulling them up or down to the top or bottom edges of the box.

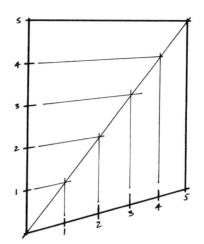

Technique

Perspective grid charts, with vanishing points and scale marks preset, accelerate the process of laying out a perspective. They limit your options for viewpoint and size of picture but, if you can work within their standard parameters, it's possible to breeze through the block-in stage of a rendering.

By simplifying the architectural details and rapidly diminishing the level of detail in the distance, this rendering was produced on a reasonable time schedule. It could easily have become an overwhelming perspective construction project. *Medium: markers, colored pencil, and acrylic on a blackline diazo print; Illustrator: Eric Hyne; Designer: LDR International; Project: Masterplan for Pennsylvania Avenue Development Corp., Washington, DC.*

How do I render round and curved surfaces?

Drawing circular shapes in perspective can prove frustrating, especially if you approach the problem armed only with an understanding of the perspective techniques used for box-shaped objects. The horizon line and vanishing points of linear perspective are only a starting point for drawing circles in perspective.

A circle, when viewed from an angle, becomes an ellipse. An understanding of the geometry of an ellipse, combined with the basic perspective principles you already know, form the key to drawing circular objects.

Two lines through the center of an ellipse, called the major axis and minor axis, define its shape. The major axis is the longest diameter of the ellipse, and the minor axis is the shortest. Both axes are always perpendicular to each other.

To demonstrate the concept of a circle becoming an ellipse when viewed at an angle, take a coffee cup, drinking glass, tin can, or other cylindrical object and hold it out at arm's length in front of you, with the top of the cup exactly at your eye level. Close one eye to see the graphic shape clearly.

When laid flat, exactly at your eye level, the top of the cup will

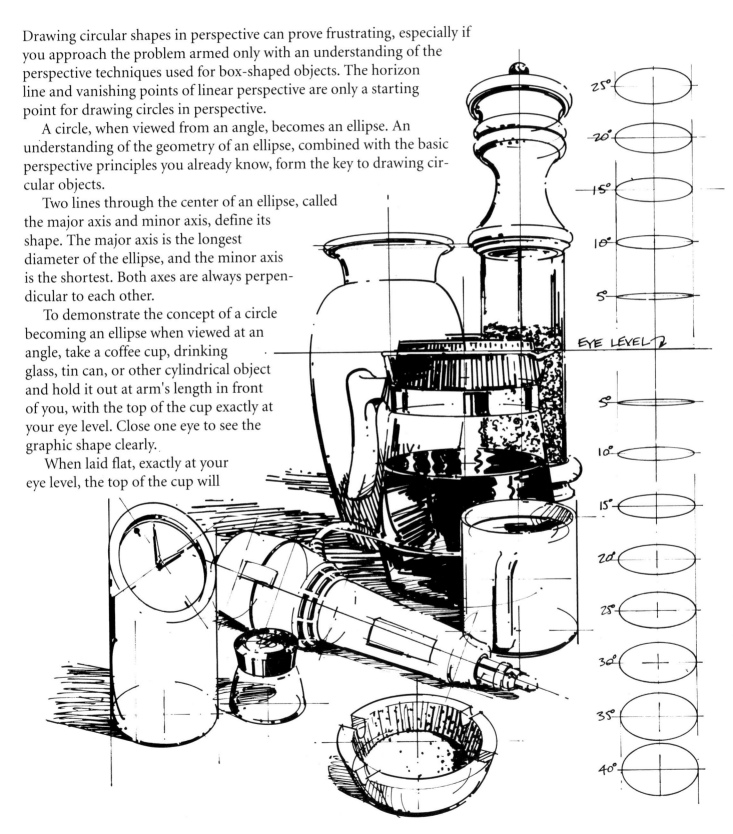

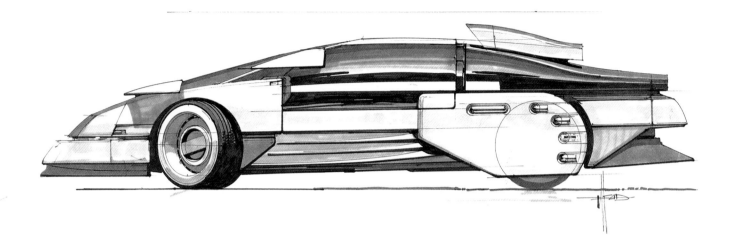

appear to be a straight line, which is exactly what a circle looks like when viewed at an angle of zero degrees. Now, slowly turn the cup toward you and watch the straight line gradually become a flattened oval. As you continue to turn the cup, notice that the major axis of the ellipse stays the same, but the minor axis grows.

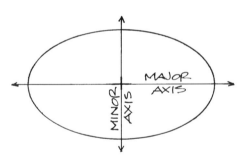

This is an important exercise, as trivial as it may seem, because it ties the theory of ellipses to your actual perception in life. Don't skip it! Take your time—remembering to keep one eye closed—and look patiently at the rim of the cup until you clearly see the enlarging ellipse shape.

Also, observe that the ellipse is always symmetrical around the two axes, and eventually becomes a full circle when it's turned perpendicular to your line of sight.

A circle fits neatly into a square in plane geometry, and an ellipse fits into a perspective representation of a square in the same way. But the positioning, or

angle at which it sits within the perspective square, is critical. If you visualize the circular shape you are trying to position as the wheel of a car, then the minor axis of the ellipse you are using to represent it with must line up with the "axle of the wheel" (that is, a line through the center of the circle, perpendicular to the plane of the circle).

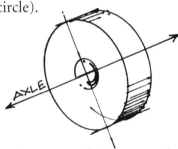

If you have a set of ellipse templates, drawing circular shapes in perspective becomes as simple as drawing a square in perspective, finding an ellipse that fits in the perspective square, touching the sides at approximately their midpoints, and then positioning it so that the minor axis aligns with the "axle of the wheel."

Ellipse template sets range from 5° to 80° of inclination, in 5° increments. The templates over 60° are rarely used for most architectural rendering situations and vary imperceptibly from a full circle, so consider skipping their purchase if you're on a budget. Another book by the authors, *Tracing File for Interior and Architectural Rendering*, provides a tracing guide for large ellipses, as an alternative to buying the larger templates.

Ellipses are sometimes necessary for elevations too. Here they are used to represent a front tire turned away from the plane of the the elevation. *Medium: ink and gray markers on vellum; Illustrator and Designer: Syd Mead; Project: preliminary study for car design.*

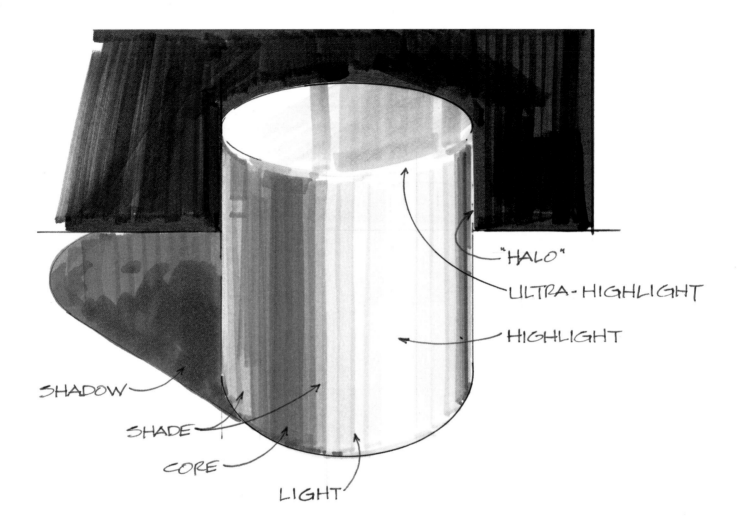

"HALO"

ULTRA-HIGHLIGHT

HIGHLIGHT

SHADOW

SHADE

CORE

LIGHT

Curved shapes that are not circular are best drawn by plotting key points along their length and connecting them using a french curve. The more points you plot, using a perspective grid as a basis for locating them, the more accurate your curve will be.

Drawing the outline of a curved shape is only the first part of rendering it, however. Representing the effect of light over its surface is equally important as getting the edges right.

Cylindrical surfaces, such as columns, are broken down into the following simplified areas for rendering: highlight, light, shade, core, and cast shadow.

The highlight is the area that receives and directly reflects the highest level of light from the light source. It is more clearly defined on a smooth surface than a coarse one, which diffuses its effect.

The highlight is surrounded on both sides by areas of direct light, which gradually fade as the cylindrical surface turns

away from the light source and blend into shade. Shade is defined as an area that receives no direct light, but does receive "bounced," reflected light.

You see, when a cylinder—or any shape, for that matter—sits on a surface, light is reflected off the surface and the background. It bounces back, returning in the exact opposite direction as the source light. Although this phenomenon is often barely discernible in real life, it is accentuated in rendering because it helps to define the form of objects in shade and adds "life" to an otherwise boring area of dark values and low contrast.

If you have ever been around a professional photographer doing a "shoot" of a fashion model, you have witnessed how important reflected light is for defining form in an elegant manner. Photographers use large reflective panels, placed behind the model and just out of view of the camera, to make sure that plenty of bounce light illuminates the shadow of a pretty face. It makes for a radiant, lively look, and the technique works equally well in rendering.

A "core," defined as the small area that receives neither direct light nor reflected light, occurs just beyond the point where light turns into shade on the surface on the cylinder. It is the darkest value on the cylinder.

At the outside edge of the cylinder on the side (or sides) where shade occurs, a "halo" of reflected light can be added. Although it must be very subtle, it is the area of highest reflected light behind the core, and helps define the perimeter of the shape against the background.

If a flat surface at the end of the cylinder is seen, then a highlight will occur along part of the front edge directly above the highlighted area of the curved surface, and the center of that area will be an "ultra–highlight" or "hot spot": an accent spot of the bright reflected light.

A cone shape is rendered in essentially the same way as a cylinder, except that all the previously mentioned areas of light and shade taper towards the point of the cone. Likewise, a round ball has all the same areas, except that they curve away from the center of the shape.

Shortcut

When you want to plot a circle in perspective freehand, it's helpful to know that a circle set into a square intersects the diagonals of the square at a point approximately 2/3 of their length from the center. Add to that the fact that the circle touches the sides of the square at their mid-points, and you are able to quickly plot eight points around the ellipse and connect them to create a satisfactory approximation of its shape.

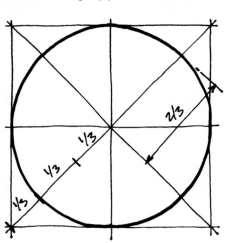 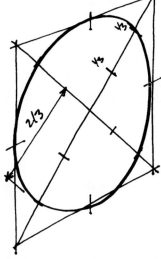

Use these points as guidelines only; it's more important that the ellipse be symmetrical around its axes and the "axle of the wheel" principle be applied to find the minor axis. Also, this shortcut only works within an area defined as a circle whose diameter is the distance between your two vanishing points. Outside of this area (in other words, at the corners of your rendering if you are using a wide viewing angle) the perspective distortions of the square you use to plot your ellipse make it too malformed to be useful.

Drawing a good ellipse freehand takes practice, so draw lots of them. Try loosely tracing accurately constructed ellipses with a single sweep of your hand to acquire a feel for the shape. It helps if you use the motion of your entire forearm to draw the lines—rather than just your wrist.

And remember that the ends of an ellipse are never pointed, no matter how narrow the ellipse. They are always rounded.

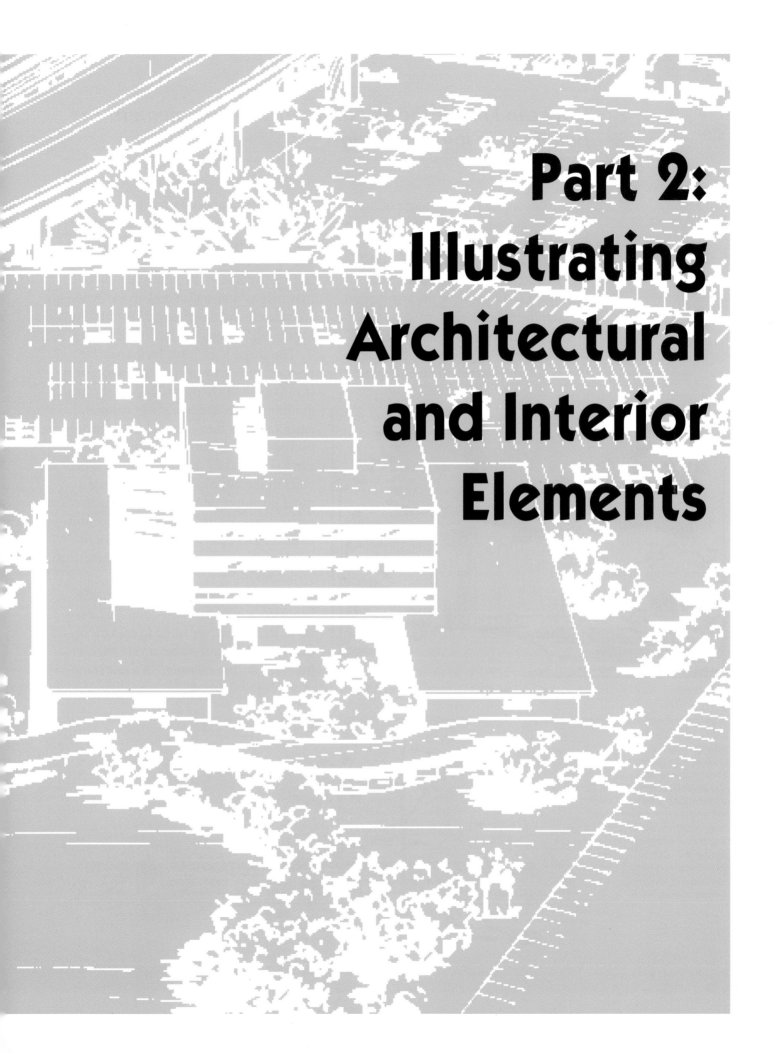

Part 2:
Illustrating Architectural and Interior Elements

How can I make the sky dramatically complement the buildings in my rendering?

Skies occupy a third or more of the area of an average architectural rendering. It's important to see them as more than just a hole behind the building: a sky is a compositional element that must be designed to complement the architecture without overwhelming it.

In a picture composition, sky falls in the category of "negative shape," an area that is not an object in the picture, but occupies space between objects.

Negative shapes are important. Try to learn to see the sky as a tangible piece of the jigsaw puzzle of shapes that make up your picture, rather than just a void. Giving that shape the name "sky piece" may help you visualize it as an entity to be considered and designed, right from the beginning, in each of your renderings.

The shape itself must be interesting; pretty clouds are only part of a successful sky. Also, skies change value and chroma, grading downward to a softer color and paler value, as they descend from directly overhead to the horizon. This phenomenon is caused by dust and moisture particles in the atmosphere, which cause a more pronounced haze at the horizon of urban areas. If you ignore this effect and paint an even, unchanging sky color, it will look flat and artificial, like a theatrical backdrop.

A sky can be peach or gray, or just a few strokes of almost any color. "The few times that I have ventured to make a sky that isn't blue have all been very successful," says Barbara Ratner. "It's just some-

A stylized representation of cloud shapes is appropriate for design sketches; to delineate them more carefully would detract from the architecture. *Medium: ink and marker on vellum; Designer and Illustrator: Michael Borne, AIA, EDI Architects; Project: Walnut Hill Shapping Center, Dallas, TX.*

thing I rarely think of trying." Your sky doesn't always have to be blue: try dawn, sunset, an approaching storm, or a nighttime sky.

Richard Radke uses pastel for his skies. "We gradate the color from a deep blue, with maybe a little purple, at the top of the picture, rubbed to a softer, pale blue at the horizon, then erase the pastel with a pink eraser to create clouds. It's some-times necessary to mask the building area to avoid smearing the blue into it. The shade of blue I use depends of the coloration of the building; we want the sky to be sympathetic to the architecture."

When composing a sky, try to use it to provide contrast. Place a light sky behind a dark building and vice versa. Also, avoid letting cloud shapes mirror the building shapes.

Dan Harmon illustrates clouds by starting with the lightest blues he can find to draw the shapes of cloud forms. "Then I begin to model them with darker colors and build them up. Basically, I make cloulds by scribbling and scrubbing".
Medium: marker on illustration board; Illustrator: Dan Harmon; Designer: John Portman and Associates; Project: Riverwood, Atlanta, GA.

An early evening sky can be portrayed graphically with a sequence of colors like these. *Medium: ink and markers on architect's sketch paper; Illustrator and Designer: Michael Borne, AIA, Selzer Assoicates, Architects; Project: Northpark Office Park, Dallas, TX.*

The sweeping cloud shapes and dramatic color gradation of the sky are used here as a counterpoint to the vertical angularity of the office tower. *Medium: marker, colored pencil and tempera on a blue-line diazo print; Illustrator: Richard Radke, Radke-Voss Collaborative; Designer: Raymond Hildreth, Architect; Project: Denver Office Building, Denver, CO.*

44

Janet Coral Campbell

Studying a sample chip under the light at your drawing table is the first step in rendering wood, according to Janet Campbell. "When I'm doing wood paneling, I like to hold the chip at different angles to see how it looks in light, shade, and shadow. Also, if it's a glossy surface, I hold other color samples up to it to see how it reflects them, so I can plan my reflections."

She develops a full–size value study on sketch paper to plan gray–scale relationships and sharpen contrasts, along with a series of color thumbnails, before beginning the final rendering. Janet prefers to work on Strathmore #210, a hot–press illustration board, using what she calls a "mix–and–match collection" of several hundred markers from four different brands.

The variations in color and value in this wood paneling give it a rich, lustrous look.
Medium: markers on illustration board; Designer: Stevens and Wilkinson; Project: Conference Room.

Medium: markers on illustration board; Designer: Stevens and Wilkinson; Project: Office Lobby.

How do I create the effect of rich, natural wood in furniture and interior paneling?

The depth of the coloration and grain in wood must be built up through several layered applications of markers and colored pencils.

First, wash most of the wood area with a highlight color (Putty or Cream, for example) that will only peek through in a few places on completion. Then, proceed with a wash of a light value of the wood color, followed by a dark value, preferably using a slightly dried marker that leaves some characteristic streaking as it is applied.

Finally, colored pencil can be used for fine–grain lines. Ideally, the grain lines should fade in and out as they move across the wood surface. If the grain lines seem too pronounced, you can go back over them in places with more marker color—the marker solvent diffuses the pencil lines slightly.

Between three and five layers of color is right for matching most wood finishes. Here's some other pointers on rendering wood:

■ Mask the wood area with drafting tape, if possible, so your marker strokes can be handled loosely without forfeiting edge control.

■ It is characteristic of any natural material like wood that both color and value changes over its surface. Don't be too consistent in applying color; try to build in gradual, but readily discernible, changes over every wood surface.

■ Sometimes it helps if you add an occasional stray spot of Lime Green or Light Violet in the first layer of color application. The subtle discoloration it adds to the final wood tone mimics natural wood flaws.

■ If the wood has a polished finish, leave an area of washed–out color highlight corresponding to a reflected light source.

Three markers formed the basis of the color, applied over a blackline diazo print, of the chest at right: Light Tan, Dark Tan, and Walnut. Putty, modified with Cream and Non-Photo Blue, was used for highlights. Also, Lime Green and Light Violet accented the basic wood colors with a little "flavoring" in places.

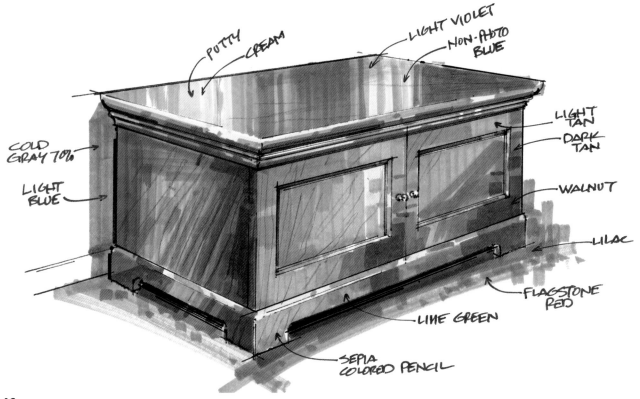

46

The end wall reflected softly in the two side walls of wood paneling gives the wood a rich sheen. *Medium: color markers on clay–coat diazo print paper; Illustrator: James Cagle; Designer: Cooper Carry & Assoc.; Project: concept for office lobby entry.*

The extreme change in value across the surface of the wood tables in this model home interior indicates a high-gloss finish. *Medium: ink and color markers on vellum; Illustrator: the authors; Designer: Cano Sotolongo & Assoc.; Project: Concept for residential development.*

How do I keep my brick areas from looking monotonous?

Consistency is a worthwhile pursuit in most endeavors but, when rendering natural materials, inconsistency is the quality rewarded with success. Nature builds changes of color and shape into stone, and unavoidable fluctuations in the clay mixture and curing temperature create color variations in brick.

Markers, on the other hand, are a medium that provides a flow of smooth, even color. So your challenge becomes to show a range of color and texture variations that simulate the natural look of these materials. Brick color variations can sometimes be handled broadly over an area, then joints added in color pencil or gouache afterwards.

Brick is often more effective when it is handled in a loose, impressionistic way, rather than carefully rendered. Medium: markers on plastic-coated diazo paper; Illustrator: Barbara Ratner; Designer: Smith Dalia Architects; Project: Sweet Auburn Curb Market.

Here are a few helpful techniques:

The rich, natural look of brick is not a single color, but a range—from yellow ochers through red–browns to brown–grays. Even when trying to match a specific brick color, variegate the brick area by adding a few strokes of wood-tone markers, such as Cherry or Walnut. Using warm grays or a pale green to subdue your brick color in a few places also enriches the surface. Touches of Grape can also be used as an accent in shadows.

Trying to meticulously render every brick is usually a mistake. Brick joints fade rapidly as a wall or floor recedes into the distance, and crisp, clear mortar lines should only be shown in the foreground.

SWEET AUBURN
Curb Market

Mortar joints are usually recessed, which is indicated by a narrow cast shadow along the bottom and one side of each brick in foreground, detailed areas. The mortar is usually best in light gray rather than white. Without the cast shadow, a foreground brick wall will look like tile.

Brick seen from a distance is more of a texture than a pattern, as in the rendering below.

Try it!

Illustrator Anthony Suminski brushes random strokes of white acrylic along the coursing of brick wall areas before applying color. The variations of the absorbency of the paper it creates makes textural effects that variegate the color slightly.

Reminder

The caps of most markers are designed to "click" closed, giving you audible assurance that they are properly sealed shut. Try to develop the habit of clicking the cap of each marker closed before you set it down on the drawing table, even when you plan to reuse it again in a few minutes. Markers are cheap to replace, but the cost of finding a critical color dried-out, with a loose cap, when you're on a deadline can be a mediocre rendering.

Brick can be implied by texture alone. After line work was completed on sketch paper, the artist placed her drawing over a sheet of rough watercolor paper and rubbed the brick areas with the side of a black *Prismacolor* pencil. Marker color was applied to a plastic-coated diazo print of the finished drawing. *Illustrator: Barbara Ratner; Designer: Roberts & Collins; Project: Schilling Plaza, Hunt Valley, MD.*

How do I portray granite and marble?

Rendering marble involves four steps: laying a wash of color, creating a mottled, soft-color from it, adding veining, then adding reflections as necessary. Granite follows the same sequence, except that the third step is adding a spatter texture instead of drawing veining.

① First, lay down a solid wash of your base color and add streaks of the secondary color. It's not critical to get an even, flat wash since inconsistencies will become part of the marble pattern.

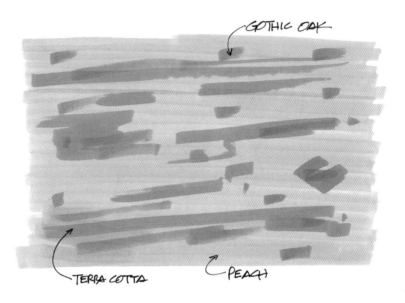

② Sprinkle lighter fluid over the color surface to create diffused spots of color. Dab with a facial tissue, as necessary, to control the pattern and move the color around.

③ Add veining lines with a colored pencil. Marble veins are not consistent--they tend to fade in and out, and also vary in width as they run through the surface--so use your finger to smudge the lines in places.

④ Finally, place reflections according to the level of gloss of the marble surface. Try to make at least some of the reflections realistic, softened mirror images of elements sitting on the marble.

Try it!

As an alternative to lighter fluid, try *Formula 409* spray for making interesting textures for marble and other effects. Mask any surrounding areas that you do not want textured to avoid overspray problems, and do not use it on any water-based ink drawings.

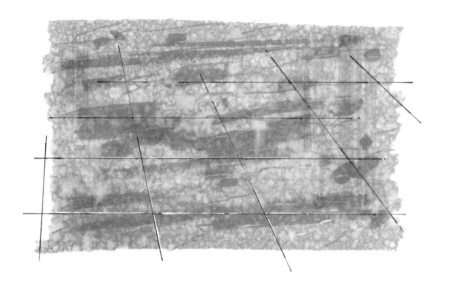

Travertine marble, chrome, glass, and carpet are all accurately represented here. *Medium: markers, colored pencil, and tempera on a blueline diazo print; Illustrator: Richard Radke; Designer: Barancik, Conte Architects; Project: Columbia Centre, Rosemont, IL.*

Anthony Suminski

"I wanted to try a simpler technique than my usual painted rendering," says Anthony Suminski, "so I switched to doing some things in markers." Anthony applies the marker color on an xerographic copy of his layout drawing made on opaque presentation film, a process available at most blueprint shops. He works in several layers of marker color, then finishes with acrylic paint for accent lines, opaque color, and textures.

For special texture situations, like brick and marble, he prepares the sur-face with areas of white acrylic paint first, before adding color. To render marble and stone, Anthony applies the paint with a sponge, dabbing to create a coarse texture, which makes the marker color puddle and absorb more randomly over the dry paint. He achieves the texture and color of brick by brushing on small dabs of white acrylic at random over the surface, along the line of coursing of the brick, leaving plenty of white paper. When brick color is washed over the surface, the painted areas vary and texture the color.

Notice how Anthony has modulated virtually every building surface, adding streaks and splotches of darker and lighter tones to keep them interesting. Also, the reflections in the fore-ground pavement give the picture a freshness and sparkle. *Medium: marker and acrylic on opaque pre-sentation film; Designer: American Medical Buildings, Atlanta, GA; Project: Medical Office Building, Georgia Baptist Medical Center, Atlanta, GA.*

Medium: marker and acrylic on opaque presentation film; Project: Apartment building concept.

Medium: marker and acrylic on opaque presentation film; Project: Bank interior.

What is the best way to indicate a mirror reflection?

Small areas of mirror glass, such as a framed mirror over a dresser, can be abstractly indicated using three values of blue and a spot or two of reflected surrounding colors, as shown below.

Larger mirrors require that you show at least some of what is being reflected. Here are some things to consider when plotting realistic reflections:

■ To be glamorous, a mirror should sparkle. This means leaving at least one spot of bare white paper as a highlight, located to be a reflection of the glare from a window or lighting fixture.

■ If you delineate the mirror reflection as tightly as the rest of your picture, add a few diagonal streaks of pale blue—just a few—as a convention to define the mirror surface.

■ A reflection of an object in a vertical mirror appears to be the same distance into the mirror that the object is in front of it.

■ To simplify the process of visualizing the reflections of a mirror that occupies only part of a wall, try blocking a reflection as though the entire wall was mirrored, then finishing only the area that the mirror actually occupies (as shown in the demonstration below).

How do I render transparent objects?

The secret to drawing transparency is to both look through an object and see the object itself at the same time. Here are some pointers on how to accomplish that feat:

▨ As your eyes scan across an object made of transparent material, where the material becomes thicker in relation to your point of view and/or the surface turns away from you (such as at the dense strips at the edge of a drinking glass) there is more distortion and refraction of light. These are points where you show more of the material, its reflectance and coloration, and less of the background.

▨ Conversely, where the transparent material is thinner and/or more perpen-dicular to your point of view, the object itself tends to disappear.

▨ Edges of transparent objects tend to have abrupt changes in lights and darks, collecting colors of their background in a seemingly random way.

▨ Most transparent objects add a sub-tle cool tint, often blue, to whatever is viewed through them. Both lights and darks seen through a clear material will be nudged toward a middle value.

▨ Even transparent objects cast a shadow, although subdued and pale.

▨ Strong, white highlights and areas of soft glare, along with low-key reflections of the surrounding environments, are characteristics to include.

Loss of detail and closer, subdued values are two characteristics of materials seen obliquely through a sheet of glass—like this cof-fee table. *Medium: ink, markers, watercolor and gouache on illustration board; Illustrator: the authors; Designer: Jacqulyn Yde Interior Design; Project: Social Room, The Waterways Condominium, Miami, FL.*

What's an easy system for indicating cars in a rendering?

Cars, like foliage and people, play a supporting role in a rendering. Architecture is always the star of the show. So, while it's important to render the basic proportions and shiny finish of a car correctly, overdoing the details and coloration distracts from your design. Keep it simple.

A full–size American luxury car, such as a Cadillac or Lincoln, measures 15 to 16 feet long, about 6 feet wide, and 4 feet 6 inches high. The height stays constant for most cars; but a mid–size car (the most common on the road today) shrinks to 14 feet long and 5 feet 6 inches wide. A compact car, such as the Nissan

Sentra, decreases further to 13 feet long and 5 feet wide.

The 4 foot 6 inch height from the pavement to the roof of a car can be subdivided into equal thirds, with 1 foot 6 inches being the approximate height of the top of the bumper, and 3 feet being the top of the hood.

Here's a few more pointers for drawing a believable car:

■ Note that the front wheels are very close to the front of the car, just behind the return of the front bumper, while the rear wheels sit significantly further in from the back bumper.

■ Observe the way all the planes of a car body curve and slope. No surface is simply horizontal or vertical. So, while you may utilize simple block shapes to develop the mass of the car, when you do the finished drawing be sure to make the hood and trunk lid slope downward from the center of the car, and the side body panels slope inward in both directions from the center body molding. All the glass panels slope inward also, especially the windshield, and all edges are rounded.

■ The side of car tires is not flush with

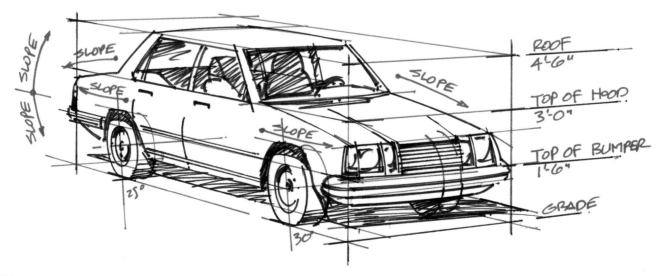

the side body panels. They are set in a little, and the body always casts a shadow on the tires.

◻ On a sunny day, the roof, trunk, and hood of a car reflect the bright sky. This washes out a lot of the body color, creating a cool, light tint of the car's color on these surfaces.

◻ Also, from a standing eye–level, the hood reflects a slice of the front windshield where they meet. The trunk lid shows a similar reflection of the back window.

◻ The part of a car's cast shadow that is directly under a car is extra dark, because no "fill" light bounces into it.

◻ The part of the side body panel below the center molding tends to reflect the pavement color.

◻ The minor axis of the ellipse you use to draw the car tires should align with the axle of the car. See Question #11 for further information on this principle.

◻ Indicate some see–through into the interior of the car, with a partial silhouette of the seats, but also let part of the glass be reflective.

◻ When drawing a row of cars in a parking lot, don't use the same style for all of them. It creates a cookie–cutter look. Give some cars a fast–back rear detail, add a few compacts and station wagons, plus perhaps a truck, and make sure that some cars are a little more forward or back in their space than others, and leave a few empty parking spaces.

◻ Keep the level of detail and drawing style of the cars in your rendering consistent with the rest of your picture. They should not contain more detail, stronger contrasts, or brighter color than other elements. If anything, your cars should be more subdued.

When working directly from photographic reference, some illustrators even delete distinctive details so that their cars are not recognizable as a specific model or brand.

Cars are carefully drawn but not overly detailed in this rendering. They add scale and movement to the picture without attracting too much attention. Medium: marker and acrylic on opaque presentation film; Illustrator: Anthony Suminski; Project: preliminary concept for a medical clinic.

Buy a copy of one of the annual automobile "buyer's guides," available at newsstands, as an easy way to assemble a collection of reference photos of late–model cars for rendering entourage. The photos used in the guides are usually more conservative, distant shots of an entire car; not the difficult–to–use, extreme close–up views that are featured in most car ads.

By roughly plotting the perspective vanishing lines of a reference photo, then sizing it in an office copier and positioning it to align with the perspective, it's sometimes possible to trace your reference photo directly, as an underlay, into a rendering—like the detail of a residential design sketch shown at right.

Simplify and stylize the car, as necessary, to match the style of the rest of your rendering.

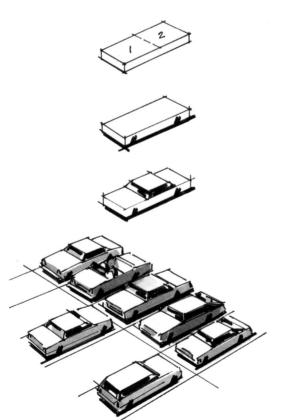

The dozens, sometimes hundreds, of tiny cars required for an aerial rendering of a suburban office or shopping complex are easy to draw, if you follow these basic steps and keep it simple:

① Draw a rectangle slightly more than twice as long as it is wide and add narrow sides to make a box shape. It should be about one-third smaller than its parking space.

② Draw a heavy line at the bottom of the two front sides as a cast shadow. Then add two heavy lines for each of the tires, setting them at an angle perpendicular to the lines which define the front of the car.

③ Add the roof of the car, slightly back from center. Since the windows taper inward on all four sides, the roof is narrower than the car and the corners of the glass angle in all around. Fill in part of the glass area with black. Taper and curve the body as an added touch, if you like. (Vary this formula for fast-backs, station wagons, trucks, etc.)

④ Add gray or a color on the two sides of the car body, a spot of blue in the window glass, and leave the top surfaces uncolored or add a very pale version of the side panel color.

"Value contrast—using the full range from light to dark—is the key to a dramatic car illustration," according to Jack Juratovic. "Basically, I do what I call a 'cartoon,' a stylized exaggeration of the reflections on the surface of the car. Then I soften it and nudge it back towards reality. You can't be subtle with reflections; they've really got to bounce.

"Chrome and black pretty much reflect all the colors that are around them," he adds. "Chrome is like a mirror—that's all it is. A black car is like a black mirror. But brass and bronze add some of the color of the product itself to the reflection.

"Your reflections also have to relate to the surrounding environment. In fact, in order for reflections on a car to look right, you need to show some of the surrounding environment, so the reflections have meaning. Show a little of what it is you're reflecting because, without that, your reflections don't mean anything."

Jack began his career as an auto stylist with Ford Motor Company, Chrysler Corporation, and his own design firm, BORT Inc.; but his passion for drawing cars led him to pursue automotive fine art full-time since 1982. He uses *Prismacolor* markers for car renderings, because he likes the way they coordinate with the *Prismacolor* pencils he utilizes for texture and color variations. Colored inks are also often worked into the backgrounds.

Notice how the bottom of the car body reflects its shadow and a little of the ground color beyond it. Glare reflected off the windshield also adds to the drama of the rendering. *Medium: markers, colored pencils, and colored inks on illustration board; Project: 2300 Alfa Coupe Prova.*

How do I portray chrome, brass, and copper convincingly?

High-gloss metals mirror their surroundings, while adding a tint of their intrinsic color to the reflection. Chrome adds a cool, light blue, while brass is tinted with a yellow ocher, and copper has a pinkish-brown coloration.

Polished metals also have a characteristic high-contrast reflection: darks are darker and lights are lighter, plus there are often abrupt value changes, but with a soft edge.

"There's a basic approach in chrome," according to illustrator James Earl, "that you start with a horizon line and reflect what is above it and below it; but the horizon is the key reference line. Chrome should impart a kind of 'watery' effect."

Other things to consider when rendering metals:

Where there is no surrounding environment to reflect, a stylized "horizon line" can be used to create an artificial environmental reflection. It should be an abrupt value change with a dark, warm reflection below and a cool, bluish, light reflection above, gradating slightly toward a middle value as they move away from the horizon line.

Don't forget that a shiny metal object also reflects parts of itself, along with the environment around it. A reflection of the handle, for example, should be visible in the body of a silver teapot.

Convex surfaces compress reflec-

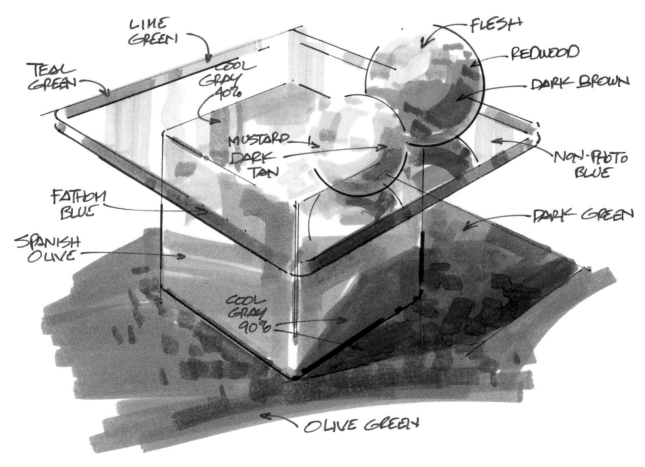

tions, while concave ones expand them.

■ Plan ahead for the position of your highlights and try to leave those areas of paper untouched and pure white. You can go back in later and tint them lightly to tone them down, if necessary, or restate them with opaque white if they have been "lost."

■ A slight, wavy distortion of the reflections in chrome adds to the metal-lic, characteristic feel of the image.

■ Avoid putting your darkest values at an outside edge of a rounded, bright metallic object. There are usually fill-light reflections there that make a subtle "halo" at the edges.

■ Portray brushed metals using a nar-rower, middle value range, with no abrupt value changes, and smoothly blended transitions.

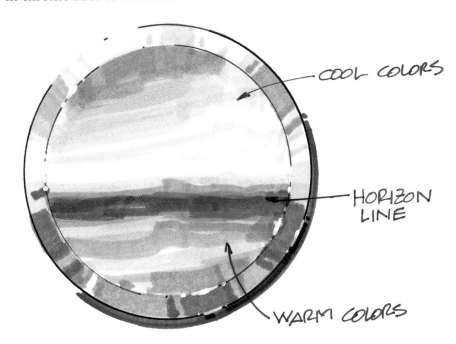

COOL COLORS

HORIZON LINE

WARM COLORS

Notice how both the chrome and black paint finish pick up environ-mental colors in their reflections, making their "sparkle" more realistic. *Medium: markers, colored pencils, and colored inks on illustration board; Illustrator: Jack Juratovic; Project: 1931 Chrysler Imperial.*

Michael Flynn.

A casual, relaxed style flows through all of Michael Flynn's architectural rendering. Besides pursuing a career as a freelance illustrator, Michael also teaches classes in Rapid Visualization at both the Academy of Art College, San Francisco, and the University of California, Berkeley Extension. "A lot of my students have already studied perspective construction techniques, and arrive at class with a very tight, calculated style. I help them to loosen up by doing 'speed drawing' exercises. We draw the same object or scene, over and over again, each time reducing the time allowed. The subject can be a magazine clipping, a design concept, or a still–life scene; but the key is to draw it several times, increasing your speed each time. On

some assignments we start at 30 minutes and work in sequence all the way down to a 5–minute deadline."

The best way for any artist to learn to work faster with markers, according to Michael, is to overcome their fear of making a mistake while putting down color. "There's no reason to panic. Just start off with the lightest colors first, building up to the darks and, if you make a mistake, you can always go back over it with colored pencils. They cover markers well on most papers, and create interesting textural effects."

For his own renderings, Michael prefers working on presentation blackline prints, with *Design Art* and *Pantone* markers, but he often experiments with different papers and mixed media.

A limited color palette and loose line drawing combine to make an elegant presentation. Notice how the black lamp shade and piano are rendered with grays on their lighted surfaces and highlights at edges. *Medium: marker and colored pencil on a blackline diazo print; Designer: Mary Leonard Interiors; Project: Residence, Palm Springs, CA.*

Trick!

If your interior rendering layouts sometimes take on a tunnel-like quality because the converging perspective lines of the floor and ceiling zoom back too abruptly, try this solution: use two horizon lines. After developing the floor elements and furniture using your original horizon line, draw a second horizon line slightly above it (but not more than 1/2"!) and move the vanishing points up to it, for drawing the ceiling elements only.

Most of Michael Flynn's renderings begin as a freehand line drawing like this. *Medium: ink on vellum; Designer: Blair Spangler Interior & Graphic Design, Inc.; Project: Hyatt Regency, Monterey, CA.*

What is the best way to portray glass?

Clear window glass takes on different qualities depending on lighting conditions. Glass backed by a dark interior will tend to reflect light like a mirror, while a light interior will make glass read as transparent. Mixing some reflective areas with some transparent areas will give your picture more life.

"Reflective glass is very easy for me to render," according to Barbara Ratner, an architectural illustrator based in Atlanta, "because I spend a lot of time looking at it in the office buildings around town, observing the effects, and I keep a photo file of different examples for reference. It's really just a sky picture on the building, with the tint of the glass worked into it." She often follows a gradated color sequence for large areas of high–rise glass, starting with light blue at the top, down to a purple–gray near the horizon, fading into a chocolate brown below—or a low–key reflection of surrounding buildings.

Unless the glass is mirror–like, the "sky picture" (or "ground picture" if you are doing an aerial rendering that looks down on the glass area) should be a cooler, grayer, and slightly out–of–focus compared to what it is reflecting. The reflection should be loosely handled, and, in most cases, it's all right to liberally revise it if necessary to help the picture composition.

Loose handling of glass reflection is easier if you let your marker color cover any window mullions and frames, and redraw them afterwards. Colored pencil

An artist's bridge, shown here, is a versatile tool that can be used for "pulling" a straight line along its length with a brush full of opaque gouache or anytime you need a surface to lean on while working on a rendering without touching its surface.

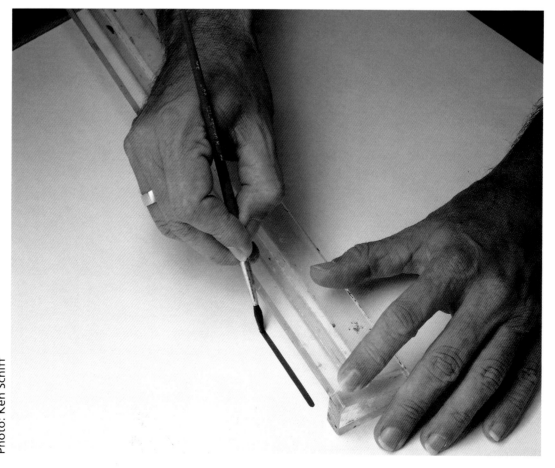

is usually not opaque enough for redrawing over markers on most papers, so a brush loaded with opaque white and pulled along the side of an "artist's bridge" is the preferred tool of professional illustrators. Like the name implies, an artist's bridge is a clear plastic tool that spans across a rendering, providing a raised straight–edge along which to pull the side of the ferrule of your brush. They are available in several lengths at larger art supply stores. If you can't find one locally, Sax Arts & Crafts, P.O. Box 50710, New Berlin, WI 53151, is a good mail–order source.

Dr. Ph. Martin's Bleed–Proof White is a popular choice for ruling lines and adding highlights to marker renderings. It's solidly opaque and marker color does not bleed up through it. Even thin lines on drafting vellum or other slick surfaces will not crawl. It does not mix well for creating tints, however, so most artists use it only as a straight–out–of–the–jar opaque white.

When drawing glass surfaces in interiors, the reflective quality is important to communicate. "I show objects reflecting in the surface, indicate a few highlights, and glaze over it all with a soft color if the glass is tinted," says illustrator Michael Flynn. "Plus, I try to pick up some of the tint of the glass in the deep green–blue color of any exposed edging of glass table tops."

The blue of the sky is pulled directly into the window glass areas and a few simple reflections have been added to create a luminous effect. *Medium: color markers on plastic-coated blackline diazo paper; Illustrator: Barbara Ratner; Designer: Cooper Carry & Assoc.; Project: Barnett Bank, Jacksonville, FL.*

BUILDING 400 - PHASE I & II
ATRIUM VIEW

BUILDING 400 - PHASE I & II
PLAZA VIEW

For an interior rendering with windows to the outdoors, the view through the glass can be "washed out" to very pale colors in the glare of sunlight to achieve the appropriate daytime light effect—except in scenes like the mall atrium view at right where sky and natural lighting dominate the picture.

Glass is treated transparently in the skylight and as a reflective surface on the store windows of this mall interior rendering. *Medium: color markers on clay-coated diazo print paper; Illustrator: James Cagle; Designer: Cooper Cary & Assoc.; Project: Prudential at Buckhead, Atlanta, GA.*

Notice how little blue is used to render the glass exterior of this office tower. Gradation of values is more important in creating the quality of reflectance. *Medium: color markers on clay-coated diazo print paper; Illustrator: James Cagle; Designer: Cooper Cary & Assoc.; Project: Cumberland III.*

Carpet can be loosely indicated by applying random stipple marks with a blunt–tip marker over a base wash of marker color. The stippling should contain several closely related colors to render the inherent color variations of carpet textures. This technique is effective for small vignetted areas, but usually looks too spotty when applied to an entire floor area.

Two more sophisticated, but time–consuming, ways to render carpet involve using pastel chalks and/or colored pencil over a base wash of marker color or using a toothbrush spatter technique.

No matter which technique you use, allow yourself the range of colors and values that make a carpet look expensive, and don't forget to make the edge of any cast shadows that fall across the carpet pick up its texture.

Also, if a carpet pattern needs to be shown, study the size and shape of one unit in the pattern and how it interlocks as it repeats across the floor. Construct a grid to build the pattern over, simplify it for the purposes of your rendering, and let the detailing fade rapidly as it recedes in space.

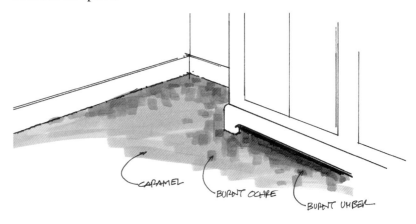

Colored pencil lines overlaying a marker wash create the texture and pattern of this carpet. *Medium: marker and colored pencil on vellum; Illustrator: Sam Ringman.*

How can I show the difference between matte and glossy surfaces?

There are two significant differences between matte and glossy surfaces. First, glossy surfaces show reflections of their environment, from subdued to very crisp and clear, depending on their level of polish. And second, there is higher level of contrast (value change) in glossy surfaces. A dull surface diffuses the light that strikes it, so values blend together and change more evenly and slowly.

Here are some techniques for defining surface finishes, illustrated below:

■ Just using vertical strokes to fill in the color on a horizontal surface is often enough to imply a glossy surface. On a vertical surface, strokes that point to one of the vanishing points help to imply the reflections of a gloss finish.

■ The edge where two surfaces meet is a convenient place to show texture differences. Don't overlook these subtle, but easy-to-use junctures. The shape of any highlights at the edge can also define surface finishes.

■ Casting a shadow across a surface and detailing the edge of the shadow is also an easy way to show textures. The shadow can be cast by a tall, unseen object outside the picture that sweeps all the way across the scene, if you like.

Tip

Most lines of markers include a "blender," filled with solvent but no color, so that you can go back into areas to refloat marker dyes and smooth out transitions. But the most effective blending technique is to overlap each new color with the previous one you want to blend it with, pulling some of the old color into the new one and working rapidly with simple, long strokes.

Blenders are useful, however, for fading out edges of color areas into blank paper. Also, pale markers such as Non-Photo Blue can be used to simultaneously blend and "flavor" areas with a secondary soft tint.

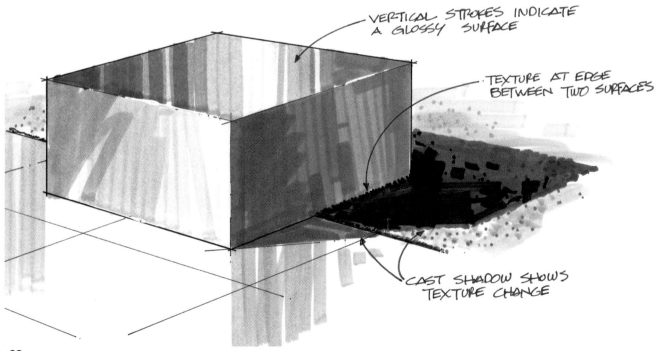

VERTICAL STROKES INDICATE A GLOSSY SURFACE

TEXTURE AT EDGE BETWEEN TWO SURFACES

CAST SHADOW SHOWS TEXTURE CHANGE

Technique

When you want a textured effect in a difficult-to-match color, try laying down a wash of marker color, then mixing gouache (such as *Winsor & Newton's Designer's Colors*) and applying it in a spatter style, with a your thumb against an old toothbrush. You can loosely mask the area to be textured by laying paper towels around the perimeter or, for a more exact mask, use a low-tack drafting tape (for heavier papers only).

The amount of paint held in the bristles determines the size of the spatter dots: a toothbrush saturated with paint will deliver large spots (appropriate for, say, a foreground stone texture), while a brush that has been shaken to remove excess paint produces a finer, more even texture. Experiment with this technique on scrap paper to get the feel for the action necessary for the texture you want. Also, be aware that a heavy, wet paint spatter will cause some buckling of thin, unmounted paper.

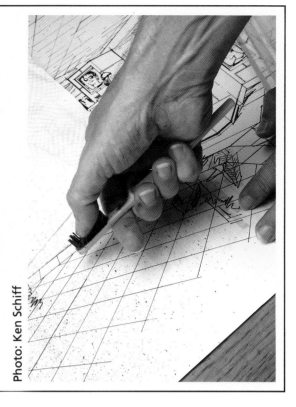

Photo: Ken Schiff

Matte, glossy, textured, and metallic surfaces are all represented in this rendering of an office interior. *Medium: marker and colored pencil on vellum; Illustrator: Sam Ringman; Project: office interior.*

"I work with a collection of about 300 markers, including several dozen of my favorite colors from each manufacturer," boasts Sam Ringman. "So the marker brand I reach for is dependent on what color I need." The one exception to his eclectic array of brands is *Pantone's* line of warm and cool grays, which he finds superior and uses exclusively.

Sam does his sketch renderings, such as the lamp drawing at right, on xerographic bond paper. "Color bleeds easily on this paper, which is perfect for a loose sketch. But, for finished renderings, I apply color to a print of the drawing on diazo blackline presentation paper. *Azon* blackline paper seems to accept the most evenly, and it's my first choice."

For the black chairs, Sam laid down solid black marker color first. "Then I worked backwards from that to develop the lighted surfaces with colored pencils," he adds. *Medium: marker and colored pencil on vellum; Designer: Sam Ringman; Project: office interior concept.*

An architectural drawing style can sometimes also be right for product illustration. This piece was developed for a brochure promoting a new lamp design. *Medium: marker and pencil on vellum; Designer: Tom Guerin; Project: Zoraida Lamp.*

Try it!

Sam never was very successful at getting an even wash of color using the special "airbrush" attachment heads for markers. "So, instead, I often use it for fast spatter-texture effects," he says. "To increase the spattering release of color, start with a juicy, fresh marker and shake it hard before releasing a short burst of air." The granite texture in the Citicorp rendering below is an example of this technique.

"People are necessary in a rendering, but they can also be distracting," according to Sam. "So I try to minimize them by drawing silhouettes whenever I can. I call them 'ghost people.'" *Medium: marker and pencil on vellum; Designer: Interprise / Southwest; Project: Citicorp signage, Renaissance Tower, Dallas, TX.*

What's the best way to depict water?

Water is easy to do as long as you remember two things: it is a reflective surface and don't overdo it. Ripples in the surface will cut into the edges of reflections, effectively editing out the details into flowing, wavy shapes of color. High value contrasts and subdued color also contribute to a liquid look.

Water is often blue, because it usually reflects a blue sky; but don't automatically reach for your blue markers. If your sky isn't blue or most of the water surface is filled with reflections of adjacent objects, then use the colors of what is reflected.

Here are a few more hints:

▨ When you are calculating reflections of objects around the edge of a body of water, remember that the height above the water level of the ground that the object sits on must also be duplicated in the reflection. Start your reflection at the level at which the water would be below the object if it was extended to meet it—as shown by the sketch below at left.

▨ As you look directly down into foreground water it is possible to see dark, cool colors, indicative of deep water; but, as your view extends up to look at water from a more oblique angle, reflections and light effects dominate.

▨ Simplify your reflections whenever possible. Just a few wavy strokes with a blunt–point marker, approximating the shape of what is reflected, are usually sufficient.

▨ The rippling effect in your reflections should get smaller as the water recedes into the distance. This is another subtle way of creating perspective depth.

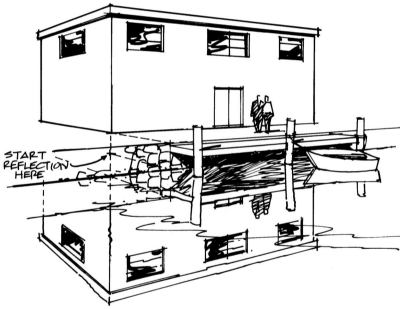

This simple approach to representing water uses the sky color directly in the light values of the water. Reflections of buildings at the shoreline are blocked in as simple shapes. *Medium: markers on plastic-coated diazo paper; Illustrator: Barbara Ratner; Designer: Cooper Carry & Assoc.; Project: Weston Town Center, FL.*

Notice that the water in the small canal is not just blue; it reflects the colors of the stone of its side wall, some the tree foliage above, the ducks, bridge, and people leaning over the edge of the water. *Medium: marker, colored pencil, and acrylic paint on a blackline diazo print; Illustrator: Eric Hyne; Designer: LDR International; Project: Big Spring Park, Huntsville, AL.*

Tip

Don't let water reflections overwhelm your picture. Too much reflection, too carefully drawn, detracts from your subject; add just enough to create a "liquid" look.

High aerial views, like this one, reflect mostly sky unless the architecture is very tall or at the edge of the water. *Medium: marker, colored pencil, and acrylic paint on a blackline diazo print; Illustrator: Eric Hyne; Designer: LDR International; Project: urban planning study for Lakeland Downtown Development Authority, Lakeland, FL.*

My drawings of people look like flat, cut-out boards. How do I make them look more dimensional?

The human figure does not have obvious, easy–to–define edges like a building. This makes people a little more difficult to draw than inanimate objects. But the answer is not to give up and just trace an outline, leaving it at that; unless, of course, your intention is to downplay and stylize your human figures.

Their forms should be rendered following the same principles as for architecture, just softened a little. People have a side which is in the light, and a side in shade (just like buildings),and they also cast a shadow. If you treat the drawing of people with the same calm, orderly approach that you use to handle architecture and furniture, they won't present such a problem.

A helpful technique to improve your rendering of the volume of the human figure is called the "Principle of the T," which is based on the fact that when one line dies into another, continuing line (as in the letter T), the first line is perceived as going behind the continuing one. It's not necessary that the two lines be perpendicular, and a series of "T" connections is more effective than just one.

Another way to keep your figures from looking like "cut–outs" is to pose them in positions where their body parts are overlapping. People also appear more dimensional when you group and overlap several figures and layer them between other entourage items.

Animated, happy people make this shopping center scene seem more inviting. *Medium: markers on illustration board; Illustrator: Dan Harmon; Designer: John Portman & Associates; Project: Northpark Town Center.*

If you find that drawing attractive, feminine–looking women is a problem, follow these guidelines:

■ Keep all lines curved, not angular, and make sure the shoulders are rounded and narrower than the hips.

■ Don't exaggerate the breast shapes; indicate them by using light and shadow shapes along the side of the form.

■ When delineating the face, use as few lines as possible. Keep the nose small and pert, and never outline the side of the nose in a front view. Indicate it by a small line under the nostrils. Downplay the eyebrows and don't cast any shadows in the eye sockets. Use a single line for the curve of the juncture of the lips, with perhaps a short line for the shadow under a pouting lower lip, if you like—but nothing more.

■ Show the mass of hair with loose, flowing clusters of lines in shade areas, with no detail in lighted areas.

Two techniques are important to Michael Borne for making a dramatic sketch rendering: establishing strong patterns of value contrast and creating a center of interest. "If you have those two worked out, a sketch will be forgiving of a lot of other problems."

The center of interest (also called a focal point) is a part of the picture that contains the main subject and that the viewer's eye should be naturally drawn to. "Each rendering should say one thing. Ideally, there should be just one message it's trying to convey. But, if there are too many elements, the drama gets lost in the competition for the viewer's attention," according to Michael.

"The longer I take and the more com-plicated I make a sketch, the more danger there is of losing my center of interest. I kind of lose sight of it. So I try to keep my renderings simple, and not overwork them, to keep my center of interest uncluttered."

Michael's second key technique, estab-lishing strong patterns of value contrast, makes the rendering crisp and easy to read. To plan his value relationships, he does a separate thumbnail study in grays before applying color to the final draw-ing. "Even the best color combinations won't work well if you don't have a good value plan. But, conversely, strange colors often look fine when they fall into a strong value pattern," he adds.

Each of his renderings begins with a

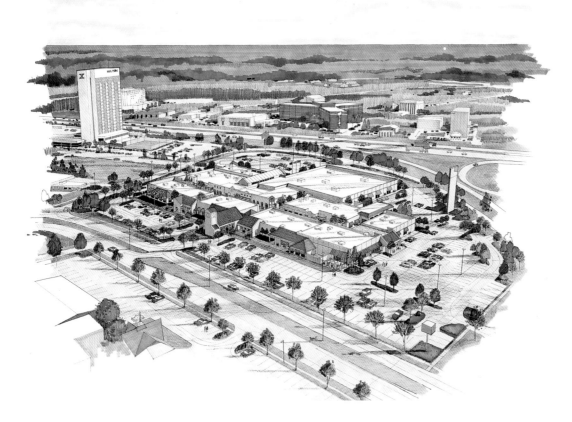

Because this rendering portrayed the remodeling of an existing shopping mall, Michael was able to work directly from an aerial photo to develop the picture. However, the surroundings were simplified to avoid any distraction from the new design features. *Medium: Markers and colored pencil on a blackline diazo presentation print; Designer: Michael Borne, AIA, Selzer Associates Architects; Project: Renovation of Esplanade Mall, Baton Rouge, LA.*

The understated line drawing and flat color of this mall interior sketch were inspired by Michael's mentor, Gordon Cullen, architect and author of the book *Townscape*. "Gordon is my all-time delineation hero. Through his technique of serial sketches, I learned how to 'see' with a pen." *Medium: Markers applied to a matte finish photostat of a line drawing; Designer: Michael Borne, AIA, Selzer Associates Architects; Project: The Springs, Dallas, TX.*

5 LEMMONWOOD MALL

loose freehand sketch, and Borne does several until he finds a viewpoint and picture composition he likes. Then he builds a series of overlays to develop and refine the picture. At the second or third overlay he switches from freehand to using a straightedge, establishes a vanishing–point pin, and mechanically constructs the perspective—as a direct overlay to his preliminary study. "If I'm short on time, I will add color and mount the third or fourth overlay drawing. But when I have a day or more to work on a rendering, I will wait until the fifth or sixth overlay before adding color, which gives me more time to play with the picture composition. So, basically I do overlays until I run out of time."

Michael's favorite drawing tool is a *Boldliner #F30* pen, made by *Berol*. The flexible tip makes it easy to vary line weight for a more expressive drawing. He also uses *Berol Prismacolor* and *Chartpak AD* markers for color, and favors *Letraset LetraMax* paper when not working on blackline diazo prints or photostats.

"Skies are easy to do, and they are always the first color I add to my drawings," according to Michael Borne. "Ideally, they contribute to the mood or focal point of the picture. The trick is to do them simply and let the white of the paper work for you. If the sky is the first color you apply, you have a built–in resistance to getting it too dark and over-worked, because you are comparing it only to the white paper." *Medium: Markers applied to a matte finish photostat of a line drawing; Designer: Michael Borne, AIA, Selzer Associates Architects; Project: The Springs, Dallas, TX.*

4 SPRINGS LAKE

The loose indication of cars in the foreground does not overwhelm the architecture. *Medium: markers on sketch paper; Illustrator and Designer: Michael Borne, AIA; Project: Northpark Office Park, Dallas, TX.*

People do not have to be drawn perfectly for casual sketches like this one. But notice that each person is in the midst of moving or gesturing—which adds life to the rendering. Medium: markers over a blackline diazo print; Illustrator and Designer: Michael Borne, AIA; Project: Lewisville Municipal Center, Lewisville, TX.

25

What are good color combinations for rendered site plans?

Color coding of the different elements of the site is the first part of what color does for a site plan. The second, and most important, contribution is a feeling of light falling across the plan. Color variations within an area can also be added to enhance the color scheme.

So, accordingly, each cluster of *Prismacolor* marker colors presented here consists of a main color or color combination, a shade and/or shadow color, plus—in some cases— one or more "flavoring" colors to create subtle changes to the main color in selected areas:

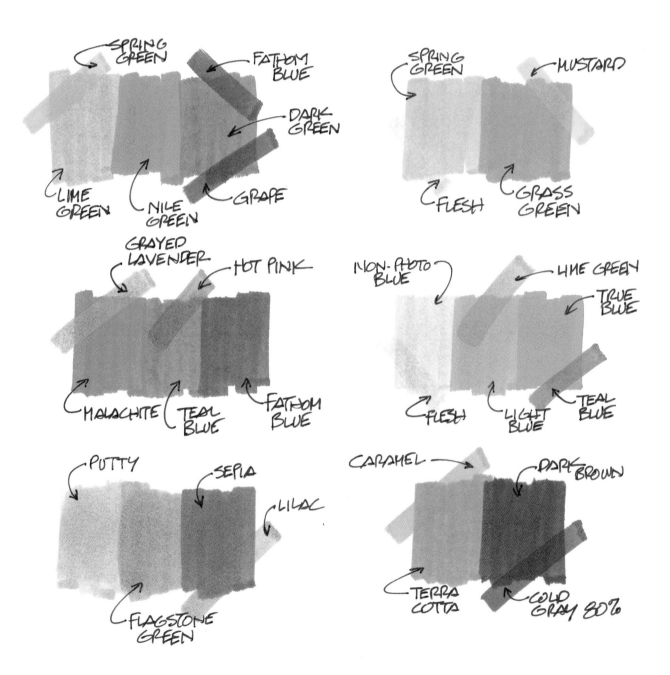

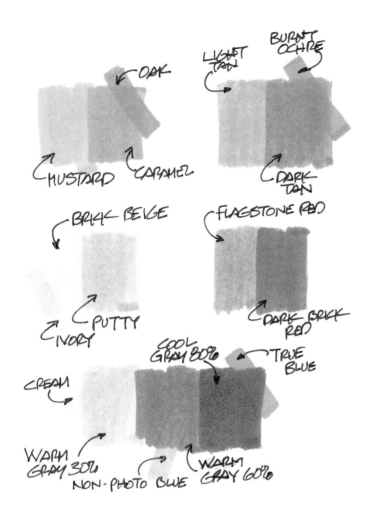

Colored pencil can be applied over markers for both texture and color variation. *Medium: marker and colored pencil on a blackline diazo print; Illustrator and Designer: Michael Doyle, Communication Arts, Inc.; Project: Boulder County Courthouse, Boulder, CO.*

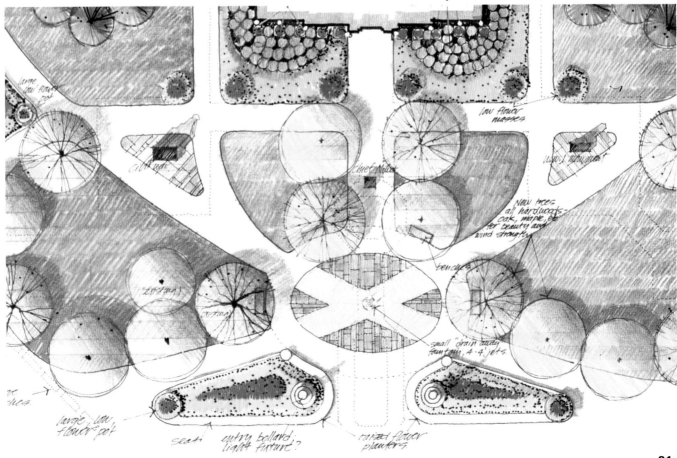

Ace Torre, a New Orleans landscape architect, uses fast washes of marker color, without any "flavoring" tints added, for his tilt-up style of site plan. To read more about this technique, see his profile on page 130. Medium: markers on blackline diazo paper; Designer: Design Consortium, Ltd.; Project: Audubon Zoological Garden.

26

How do I vary the greens to make my foliage more interesting?

One of the benefits of attractive foliage is that it can enhance a rendering without distracting from the subject. But mopping over the surface of your trees and grass areas with a bright green doesn't generate viewer interest. It's developed by the interplay of light and shadow over subtly varying foliage colors, some of which may not even be green at all.

In order to think creatively about rendering foliage, the first thing you have to do is free yourself from the obvious implications of marker colors with names like "Grass" Green or "Leaf" Green. While they are suitable to use as one of the colors in a foliage palette, so are colors like Putty and Spanish Olive.

Here are some tips for developing foliage:

 Avoid extensive use of super–bright greens like Malachite. Limit them to small areas of the middle-ground and foreground.

 Don't just vary the color of your foliage; change the value also. Try to layer light foliage between medium and darker plantings to create distinct bands of different values.

 Trees and hedges have a top, front, side, and bottom surface just like any other three–dimensional object. Don't draw individual leaves; focus on rendering these surfaces in a loose fashion, overlaid with the texture of leaves and the structure of branches supporting them.

 Most landscaping material is not an opaque mass of leaves. There are see–through holes, especially at the edges, and branches exposed in a lost–and–found pattern throughout. If you don't allow for some see-through and branches, your trees will tend to look like lollipop topiary.

This detail of foreground palm trees demonstrates the use of a three-marker cluster of colors to render foliage. *Medium: markers on a blackline diazo print; Illustrator: the authors.*

Foliage is usually rendered in three values (highlight, light, and shade/shadow) for most situations, with a fourth optional color sometimes added as a dark accent for deep shadows or a "flavoring" color modifier. Here are a few easy-to-use combinations from the *Berol Prismacolor* line of markers:

(1) Willow Green and (1a) Lime Green, (2) Grass Green, (3) Dark Green, and (3a) Fathom Blue as a dark accent.

(1) Lime Green, (2) Nile Green, (3) Dark Green, and (3a) Cold Gray 90% as a dark accent.

(1) Putty, (2) Spanish Olive, and (3) Marine Green.

(1) Lime Green and (1a) Apple Green, (2) Malachite, (3) Fathom Blue, and (3a) Black as a dark accent.

(1) Lime Green, (2) Olive Green, and (3) Marine Green.

(1) Spring Green, (2) Nile Green, (3) Teal Blue, and (3a) Fathom Blue as a dark accent.

The natural variation in grass color must be depicted to give it a natural look. Lime Green, Nile Green, and Dark Green were used as the basis for the grass swale in this rendering detail. However, a couple of strokes of Apple Green were added to the Lime Green, touches of Olive Green modified the the Nile Green, and Fathom Blue was added to the shadow area. Putty, Cream, Light Violet, Non-Photo Blue, and Mustard are a few other markers that can be used to enrich and modulate grass areas. *Medium: markers on a blackline diazo print; Illustrator: the authors.*

▨ When you want to develop highly rendered foreground foliage, separate the shade and shadow areas into two different values by adding Fathom Blue, Cool Gray 90%, Black, or Blue Violet to the deep shadows. Then add some glare highlights of almost pure white at the center of the regular highlights if the leaves are shiny. The highlights can be simply spots of untouched white paper—if you plan ahead for them.

▨ Background foliage is rendered with muted colors in a two-value scheme (light and shade/shadow only). Olive and Marine Green, Lime Green and Spanish Olive, Putty and Clay, or Spanish Olive and Clay are good combinations to consider.

Foliage is used to frame this sketch of a courtyard scene on all sides. Notice the areas of bare paper left as highlights on the fronds of the potted palm on the left. *Medium: ink and color markers on vellum; Illustrator: the authors; Designer: Cano Sotolongo & Assoc.; Project: Concept for residential development.*

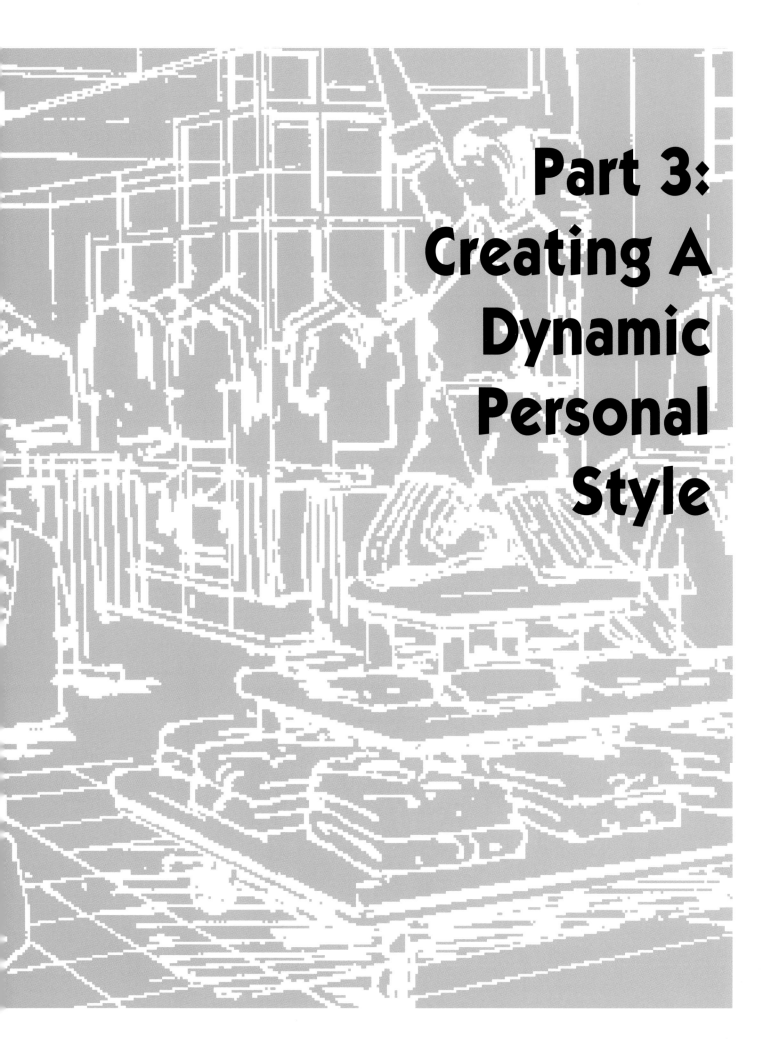

Part 3: Creating A Dynamic Personal Style

Why do most professional renderers keep a "clip file"?

There never seems to be enough time to make a rendering as wonderful as you want it to be. After the careful, laborious steps of laying out the perspective, several design conferences, and all the corrections, things tend to degenerate into a frantic rush to finish and deliver it on schedule.

But much of the dazzle and sparkle in a rendering—the elements that create magic in your viewer's eyes—comes from the entourage added near the very end of the work cycle, when time is most precious. This is where a good clip file comes to the rescue of an overworked designer. Instead of laboriously constructing the recurring entourage pieces like cars, people, and foliage from scratch, you can raid your files for items that will slip right into the picture with few, if any, alterations. And the bigger your collection of clip, the more likely you are to find a few pieces that provide the perfect finishing touches for your picture.

Also called a "picture reference file," a "swipe file," or a "photo morgue," your clip file should include:

▪ A collection of photos of architecture and interiors, especially from design magazines such as *Interior Design* and *Architectural Record*. Pick clear, well–lit photos.

▪ Examples of renderings and sketches by illustrators you admire.

▪ Photos and drawings of people, in as many different poses and situations as you can find. Keep viewpoint in mind; an eye level at about knee–high (often used for fashion photos) is not useful for most renderings. Also, try to get full–figure shots whenever possible, and avoid extremely close photos with perspective distortion.

▪ Pictures of often–used architectural surfaces such as brick, chrome, glass, and wood paneling, which demonstrate the

"Clip file" people are especially useful for interior renderings of public spaces, where realistic, contemporary figures are necessary. Medium: markers and colored pencil over a blackline diazo print; Illustrator: the authors; Designer: CLDA, Inc.; Project: department store entry concept for Mercantile Stores, Inc.

effects of light and variations in coloration over the surfaces.

▨ A random file of color swatches, photos, sketches, new products, etc., that interest you but don't fit into any regular category. Create folders with generalized names that loosely fit the subjects, such *COLORS—NICE COMBINATIONS, PHOTOS—INTERESTING COMPOSITION,* or simply *IDEAS.* If you find a particular picture fascinating but don't know what you'll ever use it for, clip it anyway and stash it in one of these catchall files. Some of the most inspirational material turns up in these odd bits and pieces.

It's important to methodically organize your reference material in files right from the beginning because, as your collection of clip grows, if you don't keep everything sorted and filed, a stack of hundreds of pictures is of little use when you're in a hurry to find a specific piece to finish out a rendering.

As your picture collection grows and the folders become swollen with material,

replace them with new, more specific categories. For example, a file simply labeled *PEOPLE* may suffice at first; but as your collection grows consider replacing it with a series of more specific folders, such as *MEN, WOMEN, SENIOR CITIZENS, TEENAGERS,* and *CHILDREN.* And when you accumulate further material, then subdivide each of those categories so that you end up with, for example, *MEN–STANDING, MEN–WALKING, MEN–SITTING,* and *MEN–LEANING.* A further subdivision might add files labeled *MEN–FROM ABOVE* and *MEN–FROM BELOW* for use in approximating the perspective effects from extremely high and low eye levels, such as aerial views or looking up at balconies.

If your volume of rendering work warrants the expense, a camera lucida (more commonly called a "lucy camera") can help you more effectively utilize your clip files. Based on optical principles originally discovered by Leonardo Da Vinci, a lucy camera uses high–intensity light and a lens similar to the kind used in 35mm SLR cameras to project an image of the flat art you put on its copy board onto your drawing surface. By adjusting the distance between the art and the lens and between the lens and your drawing surface, it adjusts the size and focus of the image.

Some lucy cameras, such as those made by *Artograph*, slide along a post mounted onto the side of your drawing board and project the image down onto the drawing. Another design, manufactured by *Goodkin*, is a freestanding unit that projects the image upward through a glass drawing surface and can only be used with translucent drawing papers. While the *Artograph* units are conveniently ready–to–use at the side of your drawing board and can be utilized with opaque drawing boards, the *Goodkin* design has twice the useful range of enlarge/reduce ratios, and the enclosure around the drawing surface reduces ambient light to make the projected image stronger.

A lucy camera enables you to size and position your reference art and trace it directly into your drawing, but in actual practice most artists trace their entourage images onto small sheets of tracing paper so that they can be overlaid on the architectural block–in and the composition can be fine–tuned by repositioning them as the drawing evolves, before the whole montage is traced onto a final sheet.

Also, it should be noted that, while a lucy camera is a great time–saver for a busy design professional, it will not miraculously solve all your problems with drawing entourage. If you can't draw well without the lucy camera, the images you produce using one will still look crude and awkward. In fact, doing further overlays, refining, and revising an image is almost always necessary to make an image derived from clip art on a lucy camera really successful. But when used judiciously as basis for further drawing, it's a great tool. And fun, too!

Some architectural illustrators, however, utilize clip files but avoid using any kind of projection device to trace the images into their rendering. "My favorite thing is to cut photos of people out of the newspaper, because I don't like the look of fashion models. I want people who are un–self–conscious," says Barbara Ratner. "And then I don't trace them. I draw them from looking at the photo, so they come out 'kinky,' a little imperfect. But it keeps me from laboring over them, which I know I would do if I traced them."

Another important reference tool that supplements your clip file is a shelf of pictorial reference books. Your library should include:

■ Any of several reference books of graphic standards and dimensions for architects.

■ Several of the books of ready–to–use entourage drawings for rendering.

■ Illustrated books on landscape foliage for your area, preferably with plenty of clear photos.

■ For interior rendering, several of the numerous "style" books, covering themes such as French Country, Caribbean, or American Farmhouse, to get a feel for the detailing and accessories necessary to create a particular look.

See the bibliography on page 142 for a basic list of suggested books. Successful designers continue to expand their pictorial reference libraries throughout their career, because they provide the jump–start of visual inspiration we all need occasionally.

Time-Saver

Clippings of interior photos from design magazines can be used to make a quick layout when showing a new design in the context of a room setting.

I want my renderings to be "loose." How can I keep them from looking stiff and mechanical?

There is a natural tendency among designers to overdo the use of outlines in drawings. After all, that's how most of us were trained: to wrap carefully drawn, even lines around the objects we describe in elevations and cross–sections.

But renderings are a different animal. A successful rendering is more impressionistic, more subjective, than a working drawing and requires a different approach. Here are some tips for loosening up your style:

■ Paint faster than you can think. It keeps your verbal, analytical left brain from interfering with your right brain's imagery.

■ The effective life span of many renderings is as short as a 10–minute pre-sentation at a corporate board meeting. This is not major fine art you're doing. Enjoy the drawing process, and know that it is only a graphic communication tool.

■ All rendering is an abstraction of reality; it's just a matter of degree. Each component of your picture does not have to be drawn as carefully and completely as everything else. Let some parts be more abstract, merely "indicated," than others.

■ Stifle the urge to construct every detail of the rendering in your preliminary studies. Instead, use a non–repro pencil (lavender for diazo reproduction, pale blue for photo reproduction) to block in the final entourage and acces-

Simple washes of marker color, applied quickly over broad areas, give this rendering a clean, conceptual look. Medium: marker on a photostat of the line drawing; Illustrator and Designer: Michael Borne, AIA; Project: The Springs, Dallas, TX.

6 HOTEL CONCOURSE

Leaving out details is an easy way to keep a drawing from becoming too fussy and tight. Here, the color of the trelles and people's clothing is left to the viewer's imagination. *Medium: markers on a blackline diazo print; Illustrator and Designer: Ace Torre, The Design Consortium, Ltd.; Project: Hilltop.*

sories directly on your final rendering. Then detail them "on the fly" as you develop the rest of the final picture.

■ Nothing works so well in a drawing as self–confidence. Make definitive marks and draw with confidence. Especially in the background, you can make just a few marks become a car, a tree, or a person "just because you say so." A slightly inaccurate, but confident line, is often more believable than an accurate, but tentatively drawn, one.

■ Remember that looseness is in the eye of the beholder. The same drawing can be too tight and mechanical for one client's tastes, and too loose to satisfy another one. Determine the level of exactness that is required for your rendering before starting.

■ Let the markers themselves keep you loose. If you work with a bullet-tip drawing pen, like the *Pentel SignPen*, and only use wide nib markers for color, you won't have to worry about getting too picky with your drawing because it's not possible.

■ Use "lost" and "found" edges to generate more vitality in your picture. This means that an edge running between two objects in your rendering can be clearly defined (or "found") at some points along its length and blurred or undefined (or "lost") at other areas.

■ Go easy on the line work early in the development of a final rendering. You can always add more after the marker color has been applied if you still feel you need it.

Try This!

The pressures of trying to render a sophisticated, elegant design to meet current architectural tastes can sometimes cause you to be too self–conscious and mechanical in your work. One way to "loosen up" is to render a tacky design where the only goal is to have some fun. Try this project: develop a series of small concept sketches for a roadside theme restaurant, where the design is an extravagant representation of the name. It must be graphic, memorable, and capable of stopping traffic. Use one of these names as a theme, or make up one of your own: Starship Diner, Dumbo's, The Big Boot, Oink–Oink Barbecue, Paddle Wheel Palace, The Red Baron Steakhouse, 'Toon Town Trolley, Disco Duck Deli, Big Top Drive–In, The Kitsch Inn, The Dog House, or Captain Nemo's Galley. Make at least one overall view, either aerial or eye level, a separate detail of the entrance and signage, and an interior view. All your drawings should be done freehand and 8" x 10" or less in size.

One way to expand your understanding of marker rendering techniques—and loosen up your style at the same time—is to use them for sketchbook and fine art drawing. Illustrator Eric Hyne pushed the limits of the traditional architectural sketch medium of markers and tracing paper to produce this frontispiece for a design presentation package. He added tempera for the opaque areas of the flowers. *Medium: ink, markers, and tempera on architect's sketch paper; Illustrator and Designer: Eric Hyne; Project: Floral No. 2.*

Technique

If you think your drawing is too tight and you want to work in a looser, faster style, try taking the *"STRAY MARK TEST"* to evaluate your picture: if a stray mark, such as a streak from a dropped pen or an incorrect line that's left unerased, is an immediately obvious flaw—then you are drawing too tightly. Add a few intentional stray marks and redraw lines, if you have to, so your drawing isn't so "perfect," and the rest of your work will move along much faster.

Although I draw the buildings accurately in my renderings, they never seem as exciting as I want them to be. How can I make them more dramatic?

Once you develop a concept and all the exploratory drawings that help you visualize the design, it's important to shift gears mentally. One kind of mindset is required to do the early drawings necessary to develop a design, and a different one to create a dramatic picture of it after it's designed.

When doing preliminary drawings to develop a concept, you should think in an objective, exploratory way. But, once you have settled on your design and are ready to sell it to your client, you must become a visual salesperson, determined to highlight your design's strong points and minimize its weaknesses in your presentation.

The picture becomes "the thing," and

your design, no matter how precious and important to you, temporarily becomes secondary. How can you best show off your new design's virtues, the dramatic parts that make it unique and desirable to your client? Is its most important feature the ingenious site layout? Take an aerial view. A towering entrance detail? Perhaps a standing eye level view, looking up, with a third vanishing point for vertical lines. Is it set on a beautiful, tropical island site? Feature palm trees, blazing tropical sunlight, and a turquoise sea.

All of this may seem obvious, but it is often overlooked by designers who are so enamored with their creation and think that "it's a well–thought–out design and will sell itself." So they they don't take the

Leaving out all the detail and color of the foreground trees can create a more interesting composition. *Medium: marker and colored pencil on a xerographic vellum print; Illustrator: Voytek Szczepanski; Designer: Franco & Associates, Ft. Lauderdale, FL; Project: private residence, West Florida.*

An early evening sky, uplit walls, and a wet, reflective street add drama to this rendering. *Medium: technical pen, marker, and colored pencil on Clearprint #1025; Illustrator: James Earl; Designer: AI Designs Ltd., Pawtucket, RI; Project: New England Institute of Technology, Warwick, RI.*

time to package and merchandise it carefully—as any successful retailer would.

Here are several techniques for increasing the impact of your renderings:

▨ Create strong, simple patterns of dark and light. Try to add touches of light to break up large dark areas and, vice versa, dark shadows to enrich the light areas to keep the composition interesting.

▨ A path of light dramatically falling across the subject of the rendering is a simple way to create drama.

▨ The corners of a rectangular picture create arrow shapes that tend to pull your viewer's eye out of the picture. Crop them with diagonal or curved shapes that nullify their effect.

▨ If you want to communicate clearly in any situation—but especially design presentations—focus on whom you are talking to. Your audience's likes, dislikes, life outlook, and career aspirations form the basis for finding the things that get them excited. Think about what your client wants to ultimately use your design to accomplish, and try to portray that as part of the picture. If it's a retail store, happy shoppers perusing the merchandise would indicate the attainment of the owner's goals, in the same way that a peaceful view out a sliding–glass door of the sun setting over a deck and jacuzzi

might mean bliss to someone planning a vacation hideaway. Details, like the kind of car pulling up to a hotel entrance, can significantly change the tone of a picture. What are your client's favorite colors? Can you use them in the picture?

▨ What you leave out of a drawing is as important as what you put in. Leaving elements for the viewer's imagination to fill in makes a rendering more interesting. Sometimes the best things to delete from a picture are the obvious ones; leave out the obvious to let attention flow to the unique, new aspects of your design. The obvious: blue sky, green grass, skin tone, or repetitive details, for example.

▨ A rendering should be an honest interpretation of a design, but there are a number of areas where the illustrator has some latitude: you can show more mature planting, beautiful lighting and atmospheric effects, crowds of people, a

An easy way to create a dramatic focal point in a picture is to have the darkest dark, the lightest light, the sharpest edge, and the brightest color all converge in one area. It's not always possible to get all four features together at one juncture, but even three out of four will make a strong, attention–getting point.

For a more dramatic picture, place the subject at the extreme top or bottom of the picture composition, offset to the left or right.

It's possible for a rendering to be dramatic and peaceful at the same time, as Eric Hyne demonstrates here. The scene is pastoral, but the dramatic scale and dark values of the foreground trees, which frame scintillating bits of white fences and buildings that peek out from between layers of foliage and shadow, make a memorable composition. *Medium: ink, marker, and acrylic paint on architect's sketch paper, mounted over Canson gray paper; Illustrator: Eric Hyne; Designer: LDR International; Project: conceptual sketches for Beechmont Farms, Baltimore County, MD.*

change of seasons, or glistening floor reflections, to name just a few examples.

▧ Use strong foreground to enhance viewer participation in the scene. A dramatic foreground—the kind your viewers feel like they can reach out and touch—will draw them into the picture.

▧ Arrange key lines and shapes in your composition to point at the center of interest to lead the viewer's eye to it.

▧ A night scene can add drama, especially where lighting and reflectance are design features or where main usage is at night, such as a nightclub.

▧ Sometimes it pays to "overdo it." One of the authors' most successful pictures was a view of a highrise office building for an ad agency. The art director kept stressing that he wanted it to be ultra–dramatic, and we thought, "So he wants dramatic...we'll give him dramatic: let's use every cheap trick we can think of." Ironically, instead of a gimmicky picture, it turned out to be quite spectacular; probably because most artist's tricks are actually simplified versions of time-honored principles of design and composition.

▧ Always remember that the ultimate purpose of any design presentation drawing is to get the client to smile and nod approval, to say, "Yes, we want to proceed with this project," and then write you a check. Whatever is required to achieve this state of consciousness in your client is what you need to do. While this may seem a little Machiavellian to the more idealistic, it won't seem that way to the person buying your services. A satisfied client, who has received exactly what he or she wants, will only consider you a brilliant designer.

I've just finished developing a design. But now the client has moved our meeting up to this afternoon, and I need to do a perspective sketch fast. Help!

It's a peculiar thing about rendering that when you have an impossible deadline and no time to think, sometimes it's possible to produce work of amazingly fresh, original quality. Then again, sometimes it's a disaster; and the difference is often in the attitude and approach taken to a rush project.

Everyone knows that time constraints can't be overcome simply by deciding to "work faster" and hoping you can pull everything together at the last minute. But how <u>do</u> you speed up the process?

First, adjust the level of finish and detail to match the time you have to work with. The less time you have, the less detail you can add to your picture.

An easy way to eliminate time–consuming details is to use a smaller format for the picture. The time it takes to do a rendering is directly proportional to its size: small renderings take significantly less time to do, no matter what level of detail is involved. If the required presentation format is too large to accommodate a small drawing, make photographic enlargements of the completed work. Many designers produce sketches in an 8" x 10" format, especially for preliminary studies; they take on a brilliant, confident quality when the marker strokes and linework are blown up several hundred percent.

Vignetting your drawing, rather than covering all of the picture surface, also saves time.

Use people, cars, furniture, foliage, and other entourage elements to cover up time–consuming areas of the rendering that are not critical to your presentation. Add these elements early in the construction of the drawing so that you don't waste time plotting architectural details that you will cover up with entourage later.

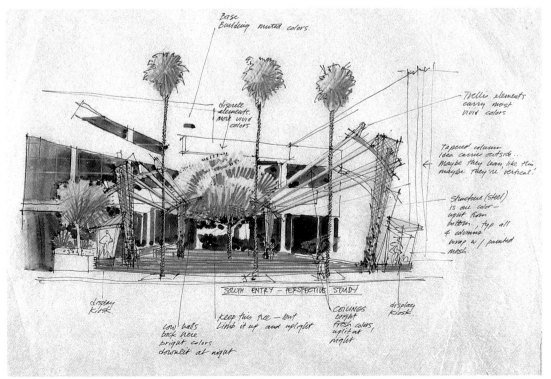

Bold colors against the solid black window shapes in the background of this sketch make a dramatic presentation out of a casual, freehand sketch. *Medium: ink line, marker, and colored pencil on architect's sketch paper; Designer and Illustrator: Michael Doyle, Communication Arts, Inc.; Project: Santa Monica Place.*

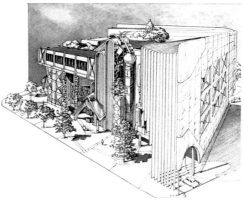

Sometimes all a drawing needs is a few washes of gray markers to frame the subject and bring it to life. *Medium: gray marker over a xerographic print on vellum; Illustrator: Voytek Szczepanski; Designer: Voytek Szczepanski and K. Talib; Project: Library design competition, Evanston, IL.*

Tip

If you don't have time to add color to your drawing, try adding gray to just one set of parallel planes within the picture. It adds some solidity to your sketch without much additional work.

Doing the final drawing freehand, loosely traced over a perspective constructed with straightedge drawing tools, speeds up the process. Drawing the entire rendering freehand, including the underlay perspective construction, saves even more time, but can be hard to accomplish when a complex structure is involved.

Always block in the large masses and shapes of your rendering first, then proceed to the secondary masses and, finally, the details. By progressing step–by–step, from large masses to small details, you gradually bring the picture into focus, which also helps you to develop the habit of working the entire picture at once and not getting bogged down in details early on. Don't spend too much time in any one area; its level of finish should not get ahead of the rest of the picture.

Often you'll find that, as you gradually build detail, values, and color over the entire picture surface, you can consider your rendering "finished" earlier than you had planned, just by strengthening the detail and contrasts in your focal point area as a final touch, leaving the rest of the picture a bit undeveloped.

Finally, and most important of all, budget your time. Divide up your limited hours, with a schedule for each phase: preliminary thumbnail studies, perspective construction, final drawing, and colorwork. At the end of your allotted time for each phase, stop, and go on to the next one. Deadlines are always easier to manage when divided up into smaller, more manageable, subdeadlines. Even if you only have a few hours to work with and you're dividing it up into half–hour and 45–minute segments, this technique will help.

Some deadlines really are impossible, and no amount of planning or shortcuts will make them feasible. But, by using these simple techniques, you may be surprised at what you can accomplish when confronted with a deadline crisis.

Medium: ink, marker, and acrylic paint on architect's sketch paper, mounted over Canson gray paper; Illustrator: Eric Hyne; Designer: LDR International; Project: conceptual sketches for Beechmont Farms, a retirement community in Baltimore County, MD.

Fast Style

The illustrator Eric Hyne, profiled on page 118, has an alternate working style that he uses when speed is paramount. "My other approach uses architect's sketch paper, and takes about one–quarter of the time," says Eric. "I develop the drawing on several overlays of paper, trying to get to the final layer as soon as I can, and working smaller than usual—about 12" by 18" or smaller."

When he has a drawing that he's satisfied with, he slips a sheet of gray *Canson* paper under the sketch and begins applying marker color. "This creates a situation where you're working from middle-tone instead of white, and I leave the gray underneath when I make my presentation. The sketch paper saturates with color much faster than other papers, and you can't get a very fine edge with the markers, so it's as if the medium is constantly reminding you, 'this is a rough sketch, this is a rough sketch.' Sometimes I need that reminder; because otherwise I'll get involved in doing little details and ruin the budget."

As a final step, he adds acrylic paint. "Sketch paper wrinkles up when I apply the paint, but I just let that be part of the style," he adds. "When the drawing is completed, I tape it, across the top only, in the center of a piece of *Canson* paper or medium–gray mat board, which leaves the drawing hanging loosely on the board." The overall effect is both dramatic and conceptual.

When time allows, Eric has the sketches dry–mounted to the *Canson* paper before applying color. Also, other colored papers can be experimented with for special effects.

Michael E. Doyle

"I don't do renderings," insists Michael Doyle, author of the popular textbook *Color Drawing*. He defines a rendering as a carefully delineated perspective of someone else's concept. "What I do is closer to 'design drawing'—developing sketches I use as a means to explore my own designs."

Michael prefers to keep his work simple and freehand. "I'm beginning to work smaller and smaller lately, and using color xerography to blow things up when they are done. Drawing smaller is essentially like using a very long pencil and standing back from the picture. This keeps my attention on the major gestures of the design, and not hung up on all the details."

AD markers, because of their extensive color range, are his favorite brand. "What I mainly use them for is to get the base gray value and base color laid in for a rendering. But it's a very flat color, so I end up using colored pencil for color gradations, texture, and just to add a little complexity to the surface."

Doyle is an associate in the firm Communication Arts Incorporated, which specializes in designing retail environments. "We do a lot of what we call

Technique

Trying to get a sketch done quickly? "When I'm in a hurry, I vignette the line work of a sketch," says Michael Doyle. "Then, in turn, I further vignette the color inside the vignetted line work, centering the color around the focal point of the picture."

By working on a gray *Canson* paper for this sketch, Michael was able to use the paper as an overall middle value, working in both directions with values: adding white pencil for lights and ink-line hatching for shadows. The cluster of people and spots of color flowing up the steps draws the viewer up through the composition. *Medium: markers, ink, and colored pencil on colored paper; Illustrator and Designer: Michael Doyle, Communication Arts Inc.; Project: Remodelling of steps at site of old "Angel's Flight" inclined railway, originally designed by Laurence Halprin, for Maguire Thomas Partners, Los Angeles, CA.*

'character development' for existing buildings, making them more user-friendly through graphic and architectural design. The critical element in the success of my design drawings for this work is creating a sense of light flooding the picture. That involves two things: using graded values and 'forcing' shadows. Forcing shadows means that, at the boundary between light and shade, the lighted side becomes brighter and whiter, and the shadow side becomes darker. Many of the great watercolor renderers of the 1920s and 30s used this technique."

A minimal amount of marker and colored pencil, placed to highlight key design features, was all that was necessary to make this sketch come alive. *Medium: marker and colored pencil on a blackline diazo print; Illustrator and Designer: Michael Doyle, Communication Arts, Inc.; Project: Santa Monica Place, Santa Monica, CA.*

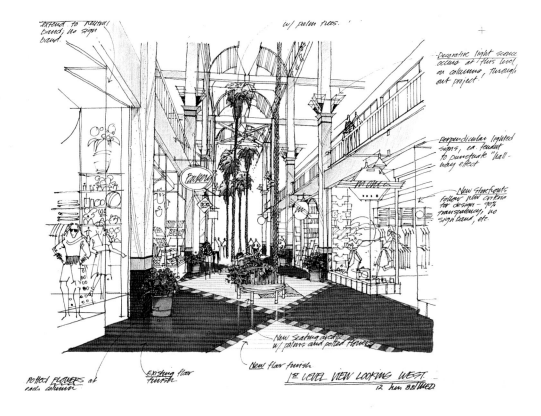

Michael uses colored pencils to gradate his marker color washes, as demonstrated here. Also, spots of gouache paint provide accent color. *Medium: marker, colored pencil and gouache on blackline diazo print; Illustrator and Designer: Michael Doyle, Communication Arts, Inc.; Project: Moor Park Center, for Urban West Communities, Moor Park, CA.*

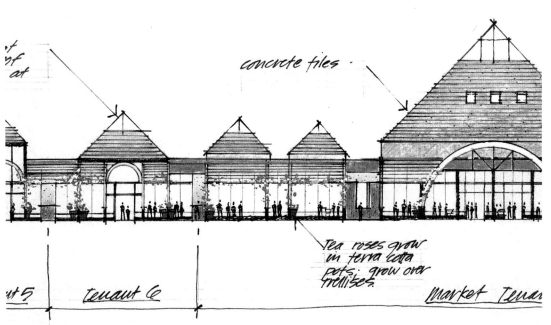

How can I check my finished rendering for errors and areas that need improvement?

Oversights and outright mistakes are a recurring problem when you're dealing with the complexities of an architectural rendering. Most designers have had the experience of working for hours on a picture, only to have someone stop by their drawing board and, at a glance, discover an embarrassingly obvious error. Sometimes you can't see the forest for the trees, as the saying goes.

The best way to overcome the perceptual problems that develop from staring at the same rendering for hours on end: put the picture aside and look at it again in a few days with a fresh outlook. However, the fast pace of today's design offices rarely allows that luxury. Most drawings are swept off the board just in time for a design meeting.

So an alternative is to trick your brain into looking at the rendering anew, from an unexpected viewpoint. Here are five techniques:

❶ Using a hand mirror, like the kind found in a drugstore cosmetics department, turn your back to the rendering and look over your shoulder at it in the mirror. The left–to–right reversal of the image will give you a new insight into your picture's merits and faults.

❷ Scan the picture with a hand-held reducing glass. Available at most art supply stores, the reducing glass is constructed like a magnifying glass; but the lens is concave rather than convex, so it creates the illusion that you are looking at your picture from a distance. It's not as effective as a mirror in uncovering oversights, but the reducing glass helps you to scan your rendering and see it as a whole, without getting up and stepping back from the drawing table.

❸ Turn your picture upside down and look carefully, especially for composition and value relationships—which should be equally strong whether your drawing is right-side-up or upside-down.

❹ Use a checklist to break down your rendering into elements that can be evaluated one at a time. A good checklist helps you to find both the glaring mistakes and the not–so–obvious faults of composition and mood that can weaken the impact of your rendering. The one that follows contains ten points that form a beginning for developing a personal checklist of your own.

❺ Also, don't forget your friend who is always only too happy to breeze by your drawing board and give you an instant critique. Those first reactions from someone who is not involved in your project can be the most helpful of all.

Remember, however, that it's unlikely that any rendering will ever fully measure up to your expectations and, if you keep fussing and picking at it, at some point the picture will start deteriorating instead of getting better. When to stop? When the picture portrays most of the things that you are trying to show and you're tired of looking at it.

McGarry's Rule

If your drawing looks right, it is right, and if it looks wrong, it is wrong. Never let your own eyes be overruled by the so-called "laws" of perspective. Even if an element in your drawing has been constructed with scrupulous, mathematical accuracy, if it looks wrong, fix it.

CHECKLIST

1 What is the purpose of the rendering? Is it for preliminary design approval, a zoning variance, securing financing, final design presentation, retail sales, or a press release, for example? Does the viewpoint, level of detail, lighting, entourage, and mood of the picture answer the questions—and overcome any doubts—that your audience has?

2 Study the rendering for any gaps where a continuing pattern or detail was left out.

3 Are there clear patterns of light, medium, and dark areas that frame the subject? Is the highest level of light/dark contrast at the focal point?

4 Are the negative shapes, such as the "sky piece," interesting?

5 Have the details been subdued, the values muted, and colors cooled in the background?

6 Have you used compositional blocks to frame the sides of the picture and arrow shapes to point to the focal point?

7 If people are used in the rendering, do they "tell a story" about the design? They should be posed and appropriately dressed to describe and enhance their environment.

8 Have you glamorized the subject, portrayed it in the best way, without being deceptive? Does your picture push the right emotional "hot buttons?"

9 What is the criticism that you most fear hearing about your work? Evaluate your picture in terms of it.

10 Is the rendering mounted and matted to enhance its sales value and your professional image? Is the drawing surface protected with a clear sealant or acetate overlay to avoid smearing and damage?

Many of the checklist items are demonstrated in this office building entry rendering by Dan Harmon. He framed the picture at both sides with people and foliage (#6), set an appropriate mood and level of detail (#1), established clear patterns of light and dark (#3), muted the background detail inside the building (#5), and glamorized the subject (#8). *Medium: markers on illustration board; Illustrator: Dan Harmon; Designer: John Portman & Associates; Project: Peachtree Center Lobby Renovation, Atlanta, GA.*

How do I "jazz up" my elevations to use them for a design presentation?

Because an elevation is a head–on view, it has intrinsic graphic qualites that a rendering often lacks. Try to keep the strong, simple shapes intact while using these techniques to enhance your presentation elevations:

■ **OVERLAPPING** of picture elements creates an illusion of depth. Try to put layers of entourage both in front of and behind your design. Position your entourage to create as many overlapping layers as possible.

■ **CAST SHADOWS** explain shape, add depth, and add graphic interest by creating strong, dark shapes. The density (darkness) you choose for your shadow areas will heighten or subdue this graphic effect.

■ **HEAVY OUTLINES** over selected edges will pop them forward for emphasis.

■ **PEOPLE**—the way they are dressed, what they are doing, and where they are standing—all explain much about your design. Make sure the people are appropriately dressed for the occasion, and happily engaged in whatever activity your building was designed for.

■ **OTHER ENTOURAGE**, such as foliage and vehicles, adds scale and further explains the functions of your design.

The layers of entourage, both in front of and behind the building, give a feeling of depth without using perspective. Medium: marker and colored pencil on a blackline Mylar diazo print; Designer: Akira Sato, The BJSS Group; Project: Murphy's Landing, Gig Harbor, WA.

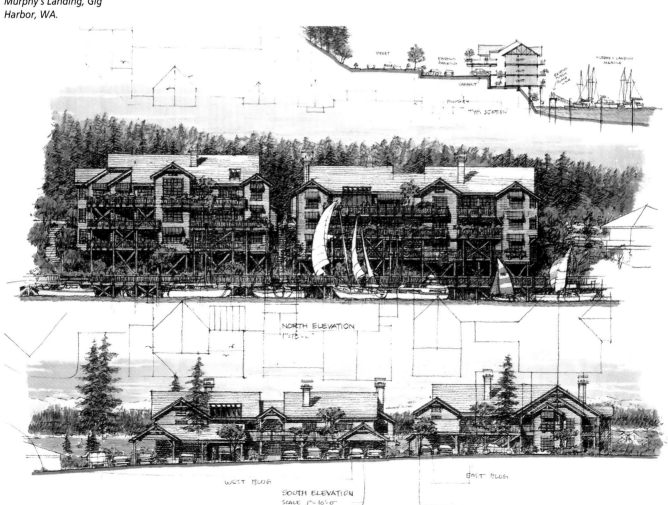

Michael Doyle first applies washes of marker color to a blackline print, then he gradates the tone in each area with colored pencils. Notice how the simple, silhouetted people animate the picture. *Medium: marker and colored pencil on a blackline diazo print; Illustrator and Designer: Michael Doyle, Communication Arts Incorporated; Project: Santa Monica Place.*

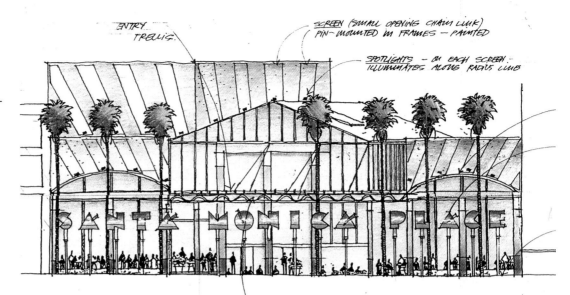

Shortcut

For a fast way to add entourage to your elevations, get *Scale Elements*, also by McGarry & Madsen, the authors of this book. It contains over 1700 ready-to-trace entourage drawings of people, foliage, and vehicles, prepared and scaled specifically for elevations.

Try This!

The time-consuming drawing of repetitive entourage elements can be eliminated by using transparent "stickyback" sheets (also known as drafting applique film) and an office copier to make duplicates of your initial drawing, then attach them to your tracing—preferably on the back, so the film is not disturbed by your continued drawing. Creating a master set of entourage drawings to reuse again and again saves even more time.

Even a product elevation like this futuristic police cruiser, stripped of entourage elements, benefits from the addition of light and reflection effects with markers. *Medium: ink and gray markers on vellum; Designer and Illustrator: Syd Mead.*

105

Akira Sato

Most of Akira Sato's renderings begin as a pen or pencil drawing on vellum, to be used as a cover sheet for a set of working drawings of one of his designs. "I make blackline prints for the cover sheet," according to Akira, "then make an extra print on *Mylar* film to use for a full-color, marker rendering." Film that has a matte finish back, satin front is preferable.

The big advantage of *Mylar* is that marker color is not absorbed into the plastic surface. Once dry, color erases easily, making it a very forgiving medium. "I have the print made 'right-reading' (emulsion side up), and apply markers to the back. Also, I work as fast as I can when filling in the larger areas of color, keeping the wet, leading edge of the color moving forward, to avoid creating streaky marks," he adds.

"But don't worry about edges when laying down color quickly like this. Whatever spills over the edge of a shape can quickly be cut back to a crisp edge with an electric eraser when you're done."

As a final touch, Akira uses colored pencils on the front surface of the mylar to highlight edges, modulate color, and create accent spots of bright color for cars and people.

Reminder

Marker color is more fugitive (susceptible to fading) on Mylar prints than other, more absorbent media. Consider making a photographic print of your rendering shortly after completion if you plan on using the image for more than a few months.

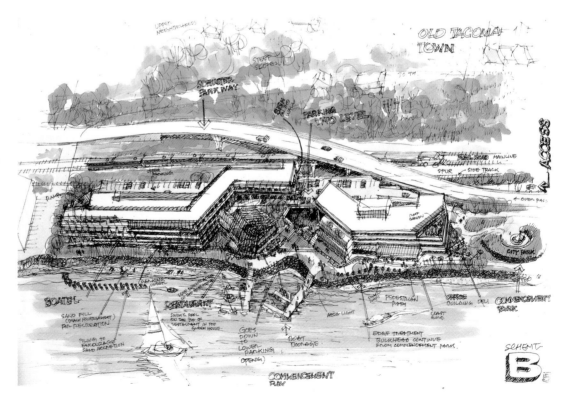

Adding design notes to a sketch rendering communicates complex proposals like this waterfront hotel complex in an informal style. *Medium: marker and colored pencil on a blackline Mylar diazo print; Designer: Akira Sato, The BJSS Group; Project: Parkshore Inn, Tacoma, WA.*

Medium: marker and colored pencil on a blackline Mylar diazo print; Designer: Akira Sato and Chris Johnson, The BJSS Group; Project: Foster High School, Tukwila, WA.

Medium: marker and colored pencil on a blackline Mylar diazo print; Designer: Akira Sato, BJSS Group; Project: Capitol Downs, Olympia, WA.

CAPITOL DOWNS
FOUNDERS GROUP, INC.
the BJSS architects/planners AIA

107

What can I do to develop a personal rendering style?

"Style is being yourself, but on purpose," according to Quentin Crisp, a British writer and film critic. It's a matter of evolution; discovering your individual, artistic signature through your work.

But how do you be yourself on purpose? In sports like golf or tennis no one expects that, if they merely study books on the techniques of leading professionals, they will soon be able to join the pro tour. In an athletic pursuit it's understood that long hours of intense practice are required to hone the motor skills necessary to have a devastating serve or perform putting wizardry. Unfortunately, rendering is often presumed by novices to be an intellectual pursuit where all that is required is extensive knowledge of per-

spective and color theory.

Mastery of rendering techniques requires the same kind of dedicated practice as any sport, music, or artistic pursuit. Keeping a sketchbook, and drawing in it regularly, is the cornerstone of developing a personal style. Great designers of the past, like Le Corbusier and Wright, kept notebooks of both visual ideas and sketches from life throughout their careers. Corbusier's sketchbooks were considered to be significant enough to be published recently, in an entire set of 12 volumes, for $500.

Save your sketchbooks for future reference. While they may not become as valuable, and pored over by scholars, as Corbusier's were, they will be a continu-

His admiration of the work of Art Nouveau artist Alphons Mucha led Voytek Szczepanski to imitate his swirling style for handling sky areas. Translated into colored pencil for the background of a modern building, however, it becomes an original statement. *Medium: technical pen, markers, colored pencil, and gouache on vellum; Illustrator: Voytek Szczepanski; Designer: A. Ericson; Project: Proposed Convention Center, San Diego, CA.*

ing source of creative inspiration for you.

Your sketchbook can also be a personal journal, with notes about your daily goings–on, aspirations, love affairs, and gossip—all illustrated profusely. By sketching both the ideas you visualize and scenes from life, you tie the two together, so that you can select freely from both in your work.

A third ongoing project to use your sketchbook for is to copy the work of renderers you admire. Don't be ashamed to copy in order to learn. Steal an idea, then make it your own by evolving it into something different. As one wag put it, "Be yourself, but in someone else's clothes."

Besides keeping a sketchbook, the other element needed to develop a strong personal style is referred to by many artists as "mileage." Unlike cars, the more miles of drawings you put on your personal odometer the more valuable your creative abilities become. Simply doing lots of rendering is the surest way to improve your style. Practicing the *right* thing is important, too; but working at the craft of rendering daily is imperative for success.

Also, a big part of what is considered "style" is the cohesive feel of a picture, the sense that somehow everything fits together. One way to enhance this is to limit your palette of markers, and repeat colors throughout the picture, in order to unify your composition. Pick up some of the architectural colors in the clothes of the people, flower colors in cars, and the like. Try to spread the use of your unifying colors in a sweep across the picture.

Any kind of limitation you impose on the structure of your picture—such as compressing the value range of your grays or only applying color with vertical strokes—creates a personal style. So experiment with different self-imposed limitations whenever you are looking for a fresh approach to rendering.

Take a handful of markers and a sketchbook along on your next vacation.
Medium: markers on sketchbook paper; Illustrator: Roy J. Strickfaden; Project: sketch of bicycle shop, Greenfield Village, MI.

Tip

If you want to get on the fast track to improving your rendering ability, consider joining the American Society of Architectural Perspectivists, also known as A.S.A.P. (an appropriate acronym for a group whose profession seems to revolve around rush projects). Their annual conventions offer seminars on advanced rendering techniques, along with a chance to meet some of the most successful pros in the business. For information on membership, write A.S.A.P., 320 Newbury St., Boston, MA 02115, or phone 617-846-4766.

Having a distinctive personal style does not necessarily require an exotic, splashy technique. Eric Hyne's careful draftsmanship and coloration create a distinctive look that is easlly recognizable.
Medium: marker, colored pencil, and acrylic paint on a blackline diazo print; Illustrator: Eric Hyne; Designer: LDR International; Project: Battleship Park, Fall River, MA.

Exercises

■ Next time you go grocery shopping, make a "visual list." Compose little thumbnail pictures of the things you have to buy; see if you can manage to do it all without writing any words or numbers on your list. Then use it to shop with.

■ Select either of the cartoon characters shown here and make a comic strip with it—at least two panels. If you can't think of a gag, take one from today's funny papers. Exaggerate gestures, use bright color markers, be silly, and have fun with the drawing. This is not architecture, so try a new approach.

■ Look through this book, and select five things you admire in the work of the designers and illustrators shown on the these pages. It could be a quality of color, blunt accent lines, a foliage texture, clustered foreground people, reflected light in a shadow...anything. Make a list, with the page where each item occurs, then compose a sketch rendering that incorporates each of the qualities you admire on your list. Don't worry about how your picture turns out, just concentrate on imitating each of the qualities you admire.

P.S.: Remember that growth as an artist is always accompanied by a least a little pain and grief. If you are pushing your sketchbook skills to the limit, trying to improve, then expect some frustration as a natural side effect of the process.

Your personal style of using color markers can easily be reinterpreted in other media. For example, these interior renderings of a luxury resort condominium were commissioned by a client who liked the boldly defined strokes of color in marker renderings, but insisted on a watercolor illustration. Square brushes were used almost exclusively, to imitate blunt-tip markers, and wet-into-wet color mixing was minimized. *Medium: watercolor on photo-mural paper; Illustrator: the authors; Designers: Cano Sotolongo & Associates; Project: Condominium complex for Ronto Development, Marco Island, FL.*

I have difficulty visualizing what I want to draw. Any suggestions?

Perhaps this has happened to you: you're working along steadily on a rendering when suddenly a little voice inside your head says "something's wrong...this picture doesn't look right," and you notice a glaring mistake in a part of the picture you have just completed. Wouldn't it be great if you could visualize ahead of your drawing hand and catch these mistakes before they happen? That same soft, intuitive inner voice can be coaxed, over time and lots of drawing, to show you the solution to your drawing problems before you blunder through them.

The first step in improving your visualizing ability is to watch a larger area of your picture as you work on it—not just the line or detail you're drawing at the moment. Instead of focusing on the line your pen is making, look at the shape you are enclosing. Let your hand continue to draw, but don't watch it—watch the overall area of the image it's creating.

With more practice, and when you become comfortable with watching the shapes you're enclosing, expand your field of conscious view to include the shapes on both sides of the line, not just the one you

are enclosing. If you can gradually, over several weeks, train yourself to your observation area this far, it will begin to seem as if your hand is on "auto-pilot" and you are not so much controlling it as watching what it does.

Remember that the shape you are making on the outside of a line (also called the negative shape) is as important as the primary shape it is enclosing. Always be conscious that you are drawing two forms, one on *each side* of your line. Keeping your gaze opened to a larger area of your rendering, and not just at the tip of your pen, is critical to letting your mind see the interrelationships of line, form, and color that make an image come alive.

Your viewers do not look at individual lines or shapes but at the whole picture. Ideally, you should develop your picture in the same way.

As a child, each of us knew this technique. If you watch children sitting on the floor drawing with crayons, they giggle with delight as a silly face appears, scream as a creepy monster emerges from the paper, and are totally immersed in the images they create. Most of us have lost this ability on the way to adulthood, carefully analyzing lines and colors to get everything exactly correct. Rediscovering the innocent urge to just watch the picture and let it develop in front of your eyes is a key that unlocks the power of your imagination to assist you in drawing.

"Don't think about it too long," advises Ace Torre, landscape architect and illustrator. "Drawing is an intuitive process and, the more you think about it, the more you complicate things and slow the process down. The critical thing about drawing is, first of all, to see; which is to acknowledge what you already look at and

This presentation sketch could be called "chocolate as architecture." To dramatize the design of a gift chocolate bar that utilized a bank's logo, it was drawn in the same close-in viewpoint and style as an aerial building rendering. The visualization skills and perspective drawing techniques of architectural illustration are easily adaptable to solve many illustration problems. *Medium: ink line and marker on* Canson Pro-Layout *marker paper; Designer and Illustrator: the authors; Project: chocolate bar for Chase Manhattan Private Bank, New York.*

visualize every day.

"If you look out the window right now and throw a rectangle around what you see, then turn that mentally into a sketch, you begin to see certain shapes and angles, how things stack and layer in relation to each other."

Ace feels that one of the biggest problems most people have with drawing is they exaggerate the angles too much, and make their perspective vanish too fast.

"In fact, most things we see in life are actually almost in elevation. Once you look at the way things occur right in front of your eyes, then you begin to trust your senses and draw more intuitively. It makes drawing much easier," he adds.

This does not mean that discipline, analysis, and self-criticism are not important to improving you rendering ability; just that they need to be held at bay when you want your imagination to soar.

"Thumbnails," the popular name for tiny preliminary studies, are a great way to rapidly explore many different viewpoints and compositional variations. They also help you to loosen up your visualization powers before launching into a full-size rendering. Conrad Booker, a Philadephia-based renderer, sometimes consolidates his thumbnails into a composition like this for client presentations. *Medium: ink on vellum; Designer and Illustrator: Conrad Booker, Ar-te-fak Design.*

Try it!

Think you can't visualize a rendering? Try this exercise before you give up on yourself: think of a person whom you have had sexual fantasies about. It could be a someone you know personally, or perhaps a movie star or famous athlete.

You have had your wish granted, and will spend a romantic weekend with her/him in a hideaway bungalow of your own design. It could be in a mountain cabin, a beach-side villa, a luxury urban penthouse—your choice! But you have to design it to be the perfect environment for your weekend. Your design can be romantic or, if you prefer, steamy and sleazy; but make it a stage set for your fantasies.

Don't put any people in these sketches. Instead, project the two of you into the layout and furnishings of the room with your imagination. Roam around the picture in your mind and fulfill your dreams in the process of drawing.

Roy J. Strickfaden

"Many students feel you must show the sky in a rendering. But you really don't; just like it is not always necessary to show the ceiling in an interior rendering," according to Roy Strickfaden, an instructor of Visual Communications at Lawrence Technological University. "The architecture is the essential part, and everything else is optional entourage. An overdone sky, one that is too blue or muddied with details, will ruin a rendering. It's better to 'suggest' a sky with a few strokes of color."

Roy also has his own design rendering practice, where he uses markers for both finished sketches and the preliminary studies for tempera renderings. He starts each rendering with a preliminary layout on canary sketch paper, which he may enlarge or reduce on an office copier before tracing it to *Crescent #300* board with graphite transfer paper. Then he develops the drawing futher in pencil before starting to apply color.

"Markers, by themselves, are not very good for detail. So I need the reinforcement of other media, such as technical pens, colored pencil, and sometimes tempera for sharp edges and thin lines," he adds.

Roy is the co-author of the book *Architectural Sketching in Markers*, a workshop-style guide to using markers for sketching and design presentations.

Tip

When working with markers on illustration board, liquid frisket (such as *Luma Liquid Mask*) can be brushed on to mask off small areas of white board when applying broad sweeps of color. It's especially effective when used with a ruling pen for the fine lines of window mullions, according to Roy, who uses the technique often.

Bold strokes of black, blunt-tip marker are used here to quickly give a feeling of solidity and light to a perspective sketch. *Medium: black marker on a blackline diazo print; Designer: Roy Strickfaden; Project: Wixom Corners*

KITCHEN
PERSPECTIVE STUDY

A limited palette of markers communicates well in concept sketches like these. *Medium: markers on black-line diazo drawing; Designer: Roy Strickfaden; Project: class demonstrations.*

My building design seems to blend in with everything else in the picture. How can I make it stand out clearly?

Use a heavy outline around important edges in an ink or pencil drawing (like the video tower below) to make them pop forward and to accentuate key shapes. But be selective, since thickening too many lines effectively emphasizes none.

Value is more important than color in creating a cohesive, easy–to–understand picture, and a simple way to organize your rendering values is to compose the picture as a kind of stage set, with three clearly defined areas: foreground, middle ground, and background. Each area is then assigned an overall value: light, middle value, or dark.

Of the possible combinations of areas and values, the most often used "staging" is foreground/dark, middle ground/light, and background/middle value—as diagrammed in the sketch at right.

Ideally, the dark foreground should have minimal value contrasts and act as a slow–moving compositional frame for the middle ground, which is bathed in a swath of scintillating light, with high-contrast shadows, plus lots of color and activity. The middle–value background then becomes the backdrop for the stage, with low–value contrast and soft edges. As the "star" of the stage composition, the middle–ground subject becomes sandwiched between the foreground and background, with the value keys making the picture easy to read at a glance.

More pointers on value–keying your picture composition:

■ Try to let each zone of value sweep across the rendering from border to border, making interesting shapes that interlock with the other two areas.

■ Lengthen, shorten, or turn the angle of shadows to suit your compositional purposes. Also, since trees, buildings, or clouds outside the picture can cast shadows into your rendering and often do in real life, you can pull cast shadows across the picture wherever they suit your purposes.

▨ If you locate your shadow vanishing point at your center of interest in the rendering, then the foreground shadows will act as pointers directing the viewer to your focal point.

▨ It is not necessary, or desirable, to clearly define every edge in a rendering. Often it's more interesting for your viewer if you let some edges of your subject blend into the background, while others are sharp and crisp. Notice how the backgrouund buildings in the rendering below blend into each other and the night sky, as compared to the sharp contrasts in the subject architecture.

▨ Try experimenting with other value combinations, such as foreground/middle value, middle ground/dark, and background/light, which can be used for a backlit subject at sunset. Always save your highest value contrasts for the middle–ground area, however, since that's where your subject is located.

Technique

When it is important to indicate a detailed background for the subject of your rendering but you don't want it to distract from your subject, do your subject in full color and the background in shades of gray or beige. This is especially effective in an aerial view, where you need to show the surrounding land, roads, and buildings but want to clearly define the area of your design.

Try it!

When you are trying to analyze value relationships—whether between different surfaces of an object or the foreground, middle ground, and background of a rendering—a gray scale strip (like the ready-to-cut-out ones on page 143) can be helpful. Hold it next to each color and squint down to assign a gray value number that it seems closest to. If the values are too close together, then you need to rework them for more value contrast.

A night scene is difficult to execute, but hard to beat when you want a dramatic picture. The ultra–dark background makes the architecture (usually well-lit) stand out in strong value contrast. *Medium: markers on illustration board; Illustrator: Dan Harmon; Designer: John Portman & Associates; Project: New York Marriott Marquis.*

hyne

"I like to render complicated spaces," explains Eric Hyne. "The kind of 'single feature' rendering, where you have one building in the center and everything goes dead as you move away from it, just doesn't excite me. It's more satisfying to look into a space with layers of foreground elements, like foliage, people, and vehicles.

"You can handle these elements in a way that is an obvious contrivance, or you can actually work out the space between the viewer and the building so that the entourage makes sense. An overhanging branch at the top of the picture, for example, looks more natural when there's a foreground tree trunk nearby that it could logically grow from and a cast shadow on the ground below it. If you take the time to develop overlapping layers of complexity in the composition, the picture will hold your viewer's interest longer."

Once the drawing phase is completed, Eric makes a black–line print and begins applying color to the unmounted paper. "Markers allow me to put down a color base that is not removable, which I can build on with colored pencil and paint," he adds. "I studied Michael Doyle's book *Color Drawing* early on, and it taught me some excellent techniques for putting down a wash of marker color down first, then adding a layer of colored pencil. I've just added an extra step in my personal style, in which I put on paint after that."

He uses *AD* markers and *Prismacolor* pencils, along with *Liquitex* jar acrylic paint, which he mixes in small paint trays with self–sealing lids that he can cap and

Try to visualize this scene without all the activity that Eric developed along the waterside promenade. Would it be anywhere near as appealing? *Medium: marker, colored pencil, and acrylic paint on a blackline diazo print; Designer: LDR International; Project: Strategic Development Initiative for the English Travel Board.*

continue to use for several weeks. "It's surprising, the tremendous amount of paint the paper will tolerate without buckling, provided it isn't used in the traditional way of applying large, wet washes," he observes.

Eric applies the paint in a creamy consistency, covering small areas at a time. The only buckling encountered is very minor, and it disappears when the paint dries. The acrylic also adheres well, and it's possible to roll the painting for shipping when it's complete.

"The picture changes dramatically when you put the paint on, because it creates the tints and white you need for highlights," Eric says. "However, don't try to hide your marker and brush strokes when you work in this medium. I used to try to blend all the colors, but it really isn't worth the trouble. It's better to just let your marks show."

Medium: marker, colored pencil, and acrylic on a blackline diazo print; Designer: LDR International; Project: Strategic Planning Initiative for the English Travel Board.

36 How can I keep my grays from turning muddy and boring?

Everything in a rendering does not have to bright and colorful. In fact, grays can act as a foil to make adjoining areas of rich color look brighter and more vibrant. They are also useful for indicating areas of low light and muted colors, to de-emphasize areas of low interest, and to frame and help focus a picture.

There are three ways to create grays using markers:

1. Reach for one of the warm or cool gray markers manufactured in values from #1 (very light) through #9 (almost black).

2. Use a ready-mixed gray with a modifying color.

3. Mix two complementary marker colors.

Technique #1 is the easiest but least effective solution. The flat, even quality of stock grays does not allow for the fact that real-life grays are richer and more varied.

Mixing a ready-made gray with a pale modifying color enriches it, introducing a little elusive, atmospheric color. It is the most efficient way to achieve richer grays.

Here are a few good choices of modifying colors to enrich ready-made grays:

When time allows, mixing complementary colors creates the richest, most satisfying grays. It requires a lot of experimentation, however, to get satisfactory results since the dyes used in markers do not mix as consistently as paint. One color often tends to overwhelm it complement instead of knocking it down to gray.

Remember to try to pick up a subtle hint of adjacent colors in your grays in order to make them fit into the picture's color scheme. Also, take into account that warm grays advance and cool grays recede when planning a composition.

Here are a few suggestions for combinations to make your own grays:

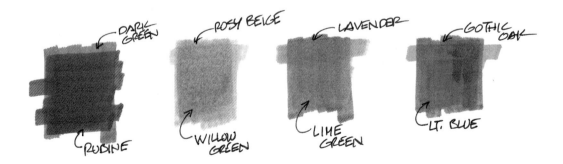

A combination of warm and cool grays—some of them specially mixed by pulling the tip and adding a few drops of dye to stock grays—are used to keep the foreground pavement interesting. *Medium: marker, colored pencil and tempera on a blueline diazo print; Illustrator: Richard Radke; Designer: William L. Carroll & Associates; Project: Montgomery Ward, Niles, IL.*

Stock grays used in limited areas with plenty of white space, as in this sketch, don't acquire the dingy look that large, unrelieved areas of gray often do. *Medium: markers on xerographic vellum print; Designer and Illustrator: Voytek Szczepanski; Project: poolside concept sketch.*

"My favorite medium is watercolor. But for projects where I can't afford to take the time, markers are great," says Voytek Szczepanski. "I use both fresh and dried–out markers, along with blenders, trying to achieve a watercolor look."

Voytek starts with a pencil layout on yellow sketch paper, from which he has an xerographic print made on vellum paper. Then he proceeds to stroke in areas of color with *Berol Prismacolor* markers, which he overlays with *Winsor & Newton* gouache and *Prismacolor* colored pencils.

"In my exterior renderings, trees are very important," Voytek emphasizes. "I go around and take photos of them whenever I can to use for reference in my renderings. Then I end up spending 60% of my time on a rendering doing the foliage, cars, and people. Only about 40% or so of my effort goes into the building itself.

"But I don't draw every leaf on a tree unless, of course, the foliage is in the extreme foreground. One mistake a lot of beginners make is spending hours and hours just drawing leaves; big leaves in the foreground, and then the same leaf shapes in the background, just smaller.

"It's silly. When you look at a tree 60 feet away, you can't see the leaves. It's just a mass shape of foliage, and that's what a rendering should portray."

A public area like this airport concourse would look incomplete without plenty of activity. *Medium: markers on xerographic vellum print; Designer: Voytek Szczepanski; Project: American Airlines Terminal, San Juan, Puerto Rico.*

Shortcut

One of Voytek's favorite techniques is to put down a layer of gray before applying the greens for distant foliage. This makes an immediate atmospheric adjustment for color. "Graying the colors as they recede in space makes my pictures more three–dimensional," he adds. "Also, the greens should be comparatively pale in background. Save the stronger, deeper chroma greens for the foreground."

Medium: markers and colored pencil on xerographic vellum print; Designer: R. Greco and V. Szczepanski; Project: Concept for reconstruction of Kuwait.

Medium: marker and colored pencil on a xerographic vellum print; Designer: Voytek Szczepanski; Project: Office Complex, Ft. Lauderdale, FL.

Sometimes my background seems to jump forward in the picture. What should I do to make it recede?

"You can push things away in the background of your rendering by making them lighter and cooler," according to DanHarmon. "It also makes a nice transition, as you move away from the focal point. Especially in bird's eye views, going to cooler blues and grays in the background is effective." Notice that there are also some violet tones blended into the background. *Medium: marker on illustration board; Illustrator: Dan Harmon; Designer: John Portman & Associates; Project: Northpark Town Center Master Plan.*

The word perspective is derived from the Latin *perspicere*, meaning "to look through," which is precisely what you want your viewer to do: look through the two-dimensional plane of your drawing surface into a scene beyond. So perspective is about making things either advance or recede in your picture, by creating the illusion of the third dimension of depth on a flat surface.

In making a rendering, getting items to pop forward is easy; making them recede into the distance is the problem. Linear perspective (using lines converging to the horizon) is only one of six different ways to create the illusion of depth, and the least effective one.

The other five, in order of importance, are:

OVERLAPPING of objects is the most effective—and underused—perspective tool of all. It occurs constantly in everyday life: if one object partially covers up your view of another object, then it is perceived as being in front of it. This simple, and obvious, observation should be utilized as often as possible in rendering. The more layers of overlapping objects you can arrange in your picture, the more depth will be portrayed.

To heighten the illusion of something sitting in the back of your picture, put several layers of overlapping objects in front of it.

VALUES SLIDE TOWARDS MIDDLE-GRAY. Light values get darker and dark values get lighter—as they recede in space. Because of this effect, it is impossible to have a pure white or black at a distance in your picture. The atmosphere between the viewer and a distant white or black color causes it to be perceived as grayed. Look at a distant skyline of tall buildings or trees and notice how gray and close in value they all are.

For architectural backgrounds to look "right," there should not be any whites or blacks in them; only middle values.

COLORS LOSE THEIR CHROMA (intensity) as they recede in space. They also become cooler. All colors gradually fade into a cool gray in the far distance, so it is impossible to have a pure, bright color like red in the background.

Use low-chroma colors for backgrounds, and cool grays for extremely distant backgrounds.

EDGES BECOME SOFTER as things recede into the distance. A sharp, crisp edge connotes a foreground element.

Keep the edges of backgrounds softer, less defined than other parts of your picture.

DETAILS DIMINISH as objects recede in the distance. You can no longer differentiate individual leaves in a tree as it moves from the foreground to middle distance, for example. In the extreme background, individual trees become indistinguishable as they merge into the tree line at the horizon.

Show only minimal detail in backgrounds.

Because you are unable to use value and color to create atmospheric perspective in a line drawing, overlapping becomes a primary tool for creating the illusion of depth. Notice how many layers of overlapped items can be arranged, even in a simple interior sketch like this one. Including the counter and pitcher with glasses in the foreground adds tremendously to the feeling of depth. *Medium: Pentel SignPen on vellum; Designer and Illustrator: the authors; Project: interior concept.*

Trick!

Each time you compose a rendering, play a little game with yourself: try to position as many layers of overlapping items as you can—going from the extreme foreground to the background, and stacking things behind each other in multiple layers. Move the items in your composition around to get the maximum amount of overlapping. It will work wonders for the illusion of depth in your picture.

Clearprint #1025 drafting vellum is James Earl's preferred drawing surface. The paper's slick surface is only marginally absorbent of marker dye, which enables him to smooth out the wet color with a facial tissue during the first few seconds after it is applied.

A clear "blender" marker will also refloat all but the deepest colors for blending. "For the stronger colors, you can put down a wash of very light gray first," he adds. "This coats the paper so that the colors stay workable and don't get blotchy."

Jim also finds that the ink line of a technical pen acts as a kind of edging device that stops the bleeding of color across the paper. When erasing any color that happens to overflow his edges, Jim refloats the color in the offending area with a colorless blender marker, then wipes or erases it away.

The finishing details and color variations are added with *Prismacolor* pencils. "If you don't modulate the color and value of large surfaces in a rendering they tend to look 'blah,' boring," Jim insists. "Colored pencils let me handle that and also be more precise in color matching."

Medium: technical pen, marker, and colored pencil on Clearprint #1025; Designer: Jeter Cooke & Jepson; Project: 100 Pearl, Hartford, CT

The extensive brick surfaces of this department store facade are treated as a texture, rather than carefully delineated mini-rectangles, and the overall effect remains realistic. *Medium: technical pen, marker, and colored pencil on* Clearprint #1025; *Designer: Arrow Street Inc.; Project: Sears, Cambridgeside Galleria, Cambridge, MA.*

Tip

When rendering brick, remember that the mortar joints are usually recessed slightly. This makes the vertical ones disappear as an angled wall recedes in space because the edge of the adjacent bricks overlaps them visually. Horizontal joints are usually stronger because the shadow cast under each brick defines them, but they also begin to break up and fade in perception as a wall recedes further. Both these spatial effects can be exaggerated to create more of an illusion of volume in your picture.

A glow of soft fill-light from the back windows gives this room a radiant, open feeling. Earl kept the shadow values in the middle range. *Medium: technical pen, marker, and colored pencil on* Clearprint #1025; *Designer: Peterson Griffin Architects Ltd. and Norman Harvey Associates, Interior Designers; Project: Cedar Pond, Peabody, MA.*

38

My design sketches of furniture seem to float on the paper. How can I make them more interesting?

When rendering a single object, you often need to add some sort of background to give the subject something to sit in front of. A simple background creates depth and eliminates the isolated, incomplete feeling of drawings without backgrounds. If you choose, it can provide a surface for the subject to cast a shadow on, giving the impression that it is solidly anchored. A background can also contain a person, a hand, or other addition to give the viewer a clue about the scale of the subject.

Here are some tips for creating backgrounds:

▨ Avoid centering the subject in the background, which creates a static composition. It's often more effective to place it off–center or partially breaking out of the background. One solution is to make the leading edge of the subject protrude past the edge of the background, as though it is popping out of a frame.

▨ Don't let the background overpower the subject. Always use a color that is subdued in comparison to the subject.

▨ Selecting a background color that is a complement to the color of the subject (opposite it on the color wheel), makes the subject's color appear more dramatic and radiant.

▨ If the object has a glossy surface, reflect some of the colors and shapes of the background in the subject.

▨ Keeping your handling of the background loose will make your careful drawing of the subject look all the more precise by comparison.

▨ For a more three–dimensional look in an abstract background, show a table edge or floor line, where the horizontal surface that the subject sits on turns into a vertical backdrop.

▨ If it's necessary to indicate a more detailed background, use silhouettes or low-contrast renderings of background objects.

The square, black background shape was placed solely to accentuate the pillow shapes in front of it. *Medium: ink and gray markers on* Strathmore UltraMarker *paper; Illustrator: the authors; Project: chaise design sketch.*

28" DIA. "VILLA POT" x 21" HIGH, IN TERRA COTTA, FROM HENRY TRELLES

Simple marker sketches were used instead of catalog cut sheets to present the fabrics and accessories for a restaurant interior. Each one has just enough background detail to give it solidity, and a surface to sit on, without detracting from the subject. Since the drawings were photograhed eleven years after completion, they also demonstrate the longevity of marker dye colors when kept out of direct light. *Medium: ink and markers on marker paper; Illustrator and Designer: the authors; Project: Louie's Backyard Restaurant, Key West, FL.*

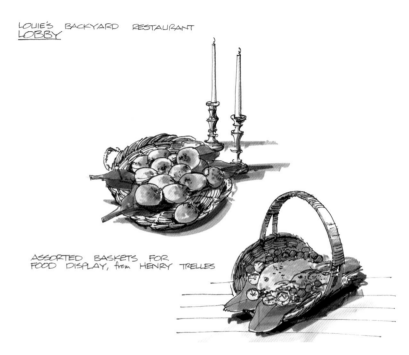

LOUIE'S BACKYARD RESTAURANT LOBBY

ASSORTED BASKETS FOR FOOD DISPLAY, from HENRY TRELLES

"TRON" FABRIC IN BLACK FROM "COUNTER-POINT"

TWO-TONE BROWN BORDER FABRIC TAPE, APPLIED

1" COQUILLE STRIE TAPESTRY FABRIC IN BROWN & BLACK FROM "BRUNSCHWIG & FILS"

L. TORRE

"Peeling the facade back from the surface of the plan" is how Azeo "Ace" Torre describes his tilt–up technique of rendered site plans. It's a simplified method of graphic communication for site designers, in which the building fronts are projected up from the plan and perspective lines are created intuitively, without the usual technical considerations.

Torre is both a landscape designer and architect, and a partner in Design Consortium Ltd., a New Orleans firm that specializes in designing zoological gardens.

"These drawings are essentially three–dimensionalized plans," he explains. "I show enough of the facades so people can see what the design delivers. Whatever you want to be the main feature of the drawing, make its vertical lines straight-up-and-down on your sheet. Then let all the other verticals around it fall away to the side of the drawing—as would normally happen in your peripheral vision anyway. This creates an automatic center of interest."

Close-ups of different areas of a tilt-up aerial site often make interest-

Cast shadows on the ground enhance the three-dimensional effect of this rendered site plan. Colors are kept bright and simple throughout. Medium: markers on blackline diazo paper; Designer: Design Consortium, Ltd.; Project: Audubon Zoological Garden.

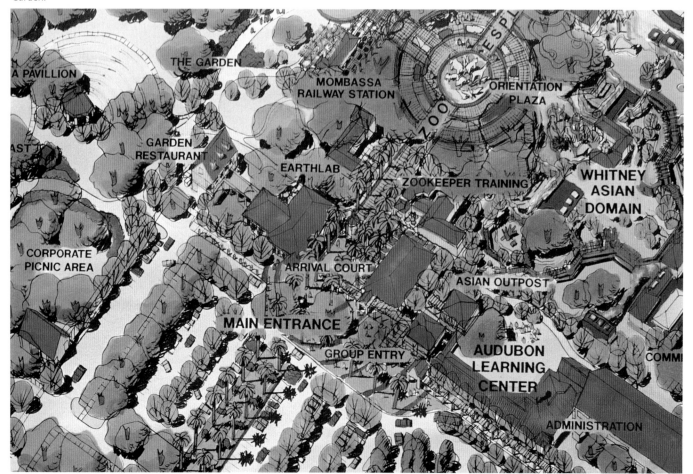

ing compositions in themselves. So, Ace has often used as many as 20 detail views of areas of a site plan to fill out a slide presentation. "Add a few eye-level sketches to that and you've got a complete design presentation."

Typically, a rendering begins with a simple base drawing done in *Pentel SignPen* on yellow sketch paper. Then a print is made on *HCP* (High Contrast Paper), a diazo paper manufactured by *James Rivers*. "The more black you put into a line drawing, the more you defeat the purpose of being able to render it with color later. So, for speed, we keep our drawings simple and use color to create the qualities we want."

The simplified, flat color and outlined people that Torre uses for concept sketches like this one speeds up the rendering process. *Medium: markers on blackline print paper; Designer: Design Consortium, Ltd.; Project: Audubon Zoological Garden.*

AFRICAN OUTPOST

Foreground trees break up the sweeping lines of the stepped seating and slow down eye movement across this sketch. They also help create a more interesting composition. *Medium: markers on a blackline diazo print; Designer: Design Consortium, Ltd.; Project: Memphis Zoo.*

131

What can I do to improve the presentation of my renderings?

Presenting a concept in the most attractive, appealing way possible is what rendering is all about. It's a kind of visual salesmanship, and taking the time to display the rendering itself with the best mounting and matting is just taking the process one step further. Dramatic presentation improves the "packaging" of your idea, and can only increase the odds of gaining client approval.

Matting can accomplish a number of objectives. By maintaining the same color and outside dimensions for all the mats in a series of drawings, for example, and adjusting the mat opening to fit the drawing, your presentation gains the continuity that a stack of drawings of different sizes lacks.

The color and value (darkness or lightness) of the mat board can even fine–tune

the effect of your rendering: mat board color will tend to accentuate its complementary color (the color opposite it on the color wheel shown below) in the rendering. Therefore, if you want to heighten the orange, gold, or brown in a rendering, use a blue mat. To enrich the red accents in your picture, mat it in a dark green.

Conversely, the mat color can be used to compensate when a color in your rendering turns out to look too bright when the picture is completed. For example, a bright green mat board will tone down the greens of foliage that is too strong. If your wood tones are too warm, use a rich brown mat, which decreases the wood effect by comparison to its deep color.

A warm gray mat will make the rendering look cooler and, conversely, a cool gray mat will make it appear warmer. A dark mat makes the values in your picture lighter by comparison, and a light mat board makes the darks appear more striking—use a black or white mat board for an extreme value contrast.

But avoid using a mat color so intense that it overwhelms your picture or looks gimmicky. If you're uncertain, buy a set of mat board corners from an art supply store, or make them yourself from scraps of the board colors you frequently use, and test the effect of different mat colors.

A sheet of clear acetate, secured to the back of your mat, will protect the surface of the rendering from the smudges and stains of pointing fingers, spilled coffee, and rubbing during shipment. It's also a good policy to use a tape hinge to secure the mat to the mounting board at the top, rather than securing it all around with tape, so that the drawing is easily accessed for changes or photography.

A label on the back of the mounting board with your name, address, and

If your completed rendering has any stray spots or smudges around the perimeter of the sheet that you want to eliminate, try Michael Borne's technique: get another sheet of the same paper that you did the rendering on, put it under the rendering, and cut out a box around the image of the rendering while simultaneously cutting through the new sheet. Then mount the rendering image sheet into the "window" created in the new sheet of paper, and tape the two sheets together with strips of clear adhesive tape in the back. Use short pieces of tape, and leave a small space between each piece, which makes the sheet less likely to buckle from moisture or temperature changes. It also makes it easier to roll the drawing for shipment. "This gives me a very clean edge for the image itself," says Michael, "and enables me to render more freely because I don't worry about stray marks or color test scribbles spoiling the picture."

phone, along with the project name and pertinent details, will assure that you get proper credit for your work. It can also help anyone who admires your rendering to contact you for new assignments.

As a final touch, if the rendering must travel any distance before being presented, wrap, tape, and package it with the same attention to detail that you gave the matting. The package itself should look impresssive and professional when it arrives. One renderer meticulously wraps all her renderings in a special blue–purple paper for delivery—even if she's just carrying them across town herself—because she wants to make a good impression from the very first moment her work arrives.

Trick!

Drawing a simple framing box around a sketch with a blunt–tip marker is an easy way to enhance your presentation. This technique is most effective for a series of small vignette drawings that are being presented mounted, without matting. The framing lines help to tie the series together, and can echo a dominant color in the design. For a lustrous accent, use a metallic silver or gold marker, as shown below.

The metallic gold box drawn around this freehand sketch is a quick way to "frame" it for presentation, and also echo the spots of gold that indicate brass detailing above the bar. *Medium: ink and markers on architectect's sketch paper; Illustrator and Designer: Jerry Szwed, Lynn Wilson Associates; Project: Sports Bar, Hyatt Regency, Orlando International Airport, FL.*

Rene Thibault

"The spontaneity of markers has always appealed to me," says Rene Thibault, a Canadian illustrator based in Calgary, Alberta. "Most of my work is in water-color. But when a client is looking for something faster or has a tight budget, then I offer my marker style. On the average, markers take me about two-thirds of the time that a watercolor rendering would."

He begins with a rough sketch to "mass-up" the form of the picture, and get an approval, before transferring it to a sheet of *Crescent* illustration board with graphite transfer paper. "First I fill in the main areas with color, working from light to dark, then begin adding line work—as a refinement, just where it's absolutely necessary—with a black fine-line marker.

Next, Rene adds colored pencil for details and texture; then a few spots of gouache for highlights. "About 95 percent of my time goes into applying the marker color and line work, and most of the remainder for colored pencil fine-tuning. Gouache I use just to add some sparkle to the picture. For example, after drawing window mullions in white pencil, I add just a spot of white gouache along their length as a subtle highlight."

Medium: marker, colored pencil, and gouache on illustration board; Project: Saddleview Square, Calgary, Alberta.

ARTIST'S CONCEPT

SADDLEVIEW SQUARE

The inherent gestural quality of a broad-tip marker line is used here to evoke a feeling of architecture without much drawing. *Medium: markers on vellum; Project: Aruba Fantasy Resort, Netherland Antilles.*

Preliminary perspective layouts have a unique dramatic quality of their own. The construction lines and blocked-in grays give this preliminary a solidity and grace that sometimes gets lost in a finished rendering. *Medium: ink and gray markers on vellum; Project: Apartment Condominium, Ft. Erie, Ontario.*

I usually don't have the time for a professional photographer to shoot my renderings before they are delivered to the client. Is it possible to take quality photos myself without a lot of expensive equipment?

Yes. With a little patience and some basic equipment set up in a corner of your office, it's possible to achieve excellent results. The secret is using the right kind of lighting and film and stabilizing your camera on a tripod.

Like most designers, you have probably tried, at one time or another, to make a simple photographic record of your design presentation before it left the studio. Using a hand–held camera and available light or a flash, the results are always disappointing: washed–out, distorted color and blurred focus make them unusable, except as a crude reference to be tossed in the job folder and forgotten.

But if you already own a 35mm single–lens reflex (SLR) camera with a normal focal–length lens, a photography setup for your studio can be assembled for approximately $450, based on 1992 prices. And, once you have the equipment, the process of positioning your rendering; adjusting the lights, exposure, and focus; and then snapping the shutter takes 10 to 20 minutes. Photographing multiple drawings takes just a few minutes more apiece. Best of all, you can shoot your work any time of the day or night—just before your design presentation goes out the door, never to be seen again.The cost per 35mm slide for film and developing will be a low 42¢, compared to the $8 to $10 that commercial photographers charge. However, since it's prudent to take several shots at different exposures to ensure that one is just right, an average cost per image will be closer to $1.50.

The process of photographing your own artwork, then critiquing the results, also helps you to draw and paint with the camera in mind. In many cases, the public will only view a reproduction of your work, not the original. So it's important to understand how the camera "sees" your rendering and adjust your colors and values to accommodate it, rather than blaming poor results on a commercial photographer.

The components you need are:

35mm SLR CAMERA…Be sure it's a single–lens reflex type, with clear through–the–lens viewing and light metering, not the compact kind with a viewfinder in the corner, used for snap-shots. Expect to pay $250 to $400 for a mid–price SLR, if you don't already have one. Your camera should have an over-ride to the automatic light–metering sys-tem, so you can adjust both the f–stop (how wide the shutter opens) and shutter speed manually.

It should also have a lens with a "nor-mal" focal length, approximately 50mm. A zoom telephoto lens that includes 50mm in its range, such as a 35–100mm lens, is a more expensive alternative to the normal lens that enables you to adjust how tightly you frame your image without moving the camera setup back and forth. Just don't use a focal length less than 50mm when photographing flat artwork, to avoid mild fish–eye distor-tions that turn straight lines into curves around the perimeter of your photo.

CABLE RELEASE…At the slow shutter speeds you will be using, a cable release assures that your camera will not be jarred by pressing the shutter button with your finger. It is a flexible tube, with a sliding cable through the center and a

137

plunger button at one end, which attaches to a special fitting usually located at the side of the lens mount on the camera body. Cable releases are made in various lengths, but 12" is suitable and costs about $12.

■ TRIPOD…Along with the cable release, a tripod enables you to take advantage of slower shutter speeds by providing a steady base for the camera. This is no place to scrimp: an inexpensive camera on a sturdy tripod takes better pictures than a razzle–dazzle camera on a flimsy one, so shop for quality and expect to pay about $120.

A good tripod doesn't settle or wobble when light pressure is applied to the camera platform while the legs are fully extended. Test it in the store before you buy. The tripod should also have two tilt axes, a bubble for leveling, and a sliding center post so the height of the camera can be changed without adjusting the legs.

■ TWO PHOTOFLOOD LIGHTS, WITH STAND…A pair of studio lights with a 12" reflector, such as the *Victor PL12*, and two telescoping metal stands, plus 500 watt ECT bulbs, rated at 3200 degrees Kelvin. All are available at a professional photo–supply house. Expect to pay about $130 each for a studio light on a telescoping metal stand, and $5 each for 500–watt ECT lamps.

If you like the industrial look, get your studio light and stand in gray or black, with a brushed metal reflector. Change the bulb to a regular soft–white one when not using it for photography, point the reflector up vertically, and you have a high–tech torchière for office decor.

■ TYPE B TUNGSTEN SLIDE FILM…Both *Tungsten Ecktachrome 50*, manufactured by Kodak, and *Fujichrome 64T*, from Fuji of Japan, are Type B films, balanced to match your 3200–degree photoflood lamps. The authors prefer Fujichrome 64T because of its higher color saturation and contrast. *Tungsten*

Ecktachrome 50 is more readily available, but neither of these films is found at drugstores or one–hour labs. They are considered "professional" films, available only at a professional photo supply.

Professional films are more sensitive to the effects of heat and age than the amateur variety. For best results, buy fresh film and, unless you plan to use it the same day it's purchased, keep the film in a refrigerator until ready to use. Allow at least half an hour for the film to reach room temperature, so there is no condensation from refrigeration on the film when you use it.

■ KODAK GRAY CARD…The white background and dramatic contrasts of most marker renderings can throw off the averaging light meter in many cameras. A more accurate way to adjust the camera exposure settings is to take your light–meter reading while viewing a specially manufactured card that reflects exactly 18% of the light that strikes it— called a "gray card." Manufactured by Kodak, a set of three costs about $10.

■ CORK OR OTHER PINUP SURFACE…A cork bulletin board, available in a 30"-x-40" size at office–supply stores for about $35, or some other wall–mounted surface that easily accommodates pushpins for securing your art flat.

Assembling all this equipment may sound complicated, but the only difficult part is finding a professional photo supply house that stocks equipment and film for commercial photographers. Most larger towns have one. If yours doesn't, look in one of the popular photography magazines for a mail–order house and order from the catalog.

Once the equipment is assembled in your studio, use the following six steps to shoot your work. As the process becomes routine, it will take only a few minutes.

① Position the rendering on a vertical mounting surface with pushpins. Made sure that it sits flat and does not bow at the center or warp at the corners. Remove any glass covering or shiny framing material to eliminate problems with glare spots.

② Set up your camera on the tripod and square the artwork so that it is positioned opposite the center of the piece and perpendicular to it. Look through the camera and, if all four sides of the picture aren't parallel to the sides of your viewfinder, adjust the camera position and angle.

③ Set up one light on either side of the art at a 30–to–45 degree angle to the wall. Position the lights almost as far back as the camera, if possible, but at least three feet from the art. If you need to place the lights far in front of the camera, turn them so no light shines directly back on the camera lens.

Switch the lights on and look through the camera for any signs of glare, or "hot spots." If you find any, try moving the lights to a more oblique angle to the wall.

④ Carefully remove your camera from the tripod, so as not to disturb its position, and check that the camera is set for the proper film speed. Turn the floodlights on, turn off any other lights in the room, and close the blinds or loosely cover any windows. Set your f–stop at 8 or 11. Hold the Kodak gray card over a corner of the picture, using one hand, and look through the camera, held in your other hand, so that the gray card fills the viewfinder. Note the shutter speed indicated by your built–in light meter. Make sure no part of your body is casting a shadow on the gray card while you are taking a reading.

Move the card over the surface of the rendering and take a reading at each position to confirm that the shutter speed reading is consistent everywhere. If it isn't, adjust the lights until you get the same reading throughout. Use the manual override to turn off your camera's automatic exposure setting feature, and set the camera for that shutter speed.

⑤ Reset your camera on the tripod and focus. Use the split–image focus on a line or edge in the picture, if possible.

⑥ Holding the cable–release plunger, gently snap the shutter. Then "bracket" the exposure by setting the f–stop one notch higher, snapping the shutter, then setting it one notch lower than the original setting, and snapping the shutter again. This gives you a range of exposures to choose from.

For the best–quality slides, the final step is to have your film developed by a professional photo lab. Many commercial labs will turn your film around in two or three hours. Another alternative, if you have more time, is to have the lab send your film to Kodak for processing. It takes several days, but finicky types swear Kodak processing is significantly better and worth the wait.

If you also need prints, have the lab make an internegative or use the Cibachrome process to make a print directly from the slide. As a rule of thumb for making a sharp print, do not enlarge a 35mm slide to more than ten times its size, which limits you to a maximum of approximately 11" x 14". Larger sizes, up to 20" x 30", look fine but show a slightly grainy texture and softer edges.

Shortcut

If all the steps involved in shooting your renderings indoors with photofloods and professional film seem too complicated for you, try photographing them outside in "open shade" (an area that does not receive direct sunlight but is open enough to get plenty of bounce sunlight from its surroundings) on a sunny day. If you don't need the control and consistency that studio photography offers, it can be an acceptable alternative.

For best results, follow the same procedures outlined for studio photography, including using a tripod, cable release, and gray card. Select a daylight-rated film with a low ASA rating, such a Fujichrome 50, for brightest colors.

Part 4:
Resources
and Index

FURTHER READING

Ideally, your growth as a designer and illustrator will continue throughout your career. Successful creative professionals consider each project as a fresh challenge, and the best rendering of their life is always "the next one."

A good way to keep your outlook fresh, with new ideas flowing, is to read how-to books on design and illustration and accumulate a library of visual reference volumes. Here are some of the authors' favorites:

Rapid Viz, by Hanks and Belliston (William Kaufmann, Inc., 1980). Simple techniques for developing your abilities to sketch and visualize design concepts.

Keys to Drawing, by Bert Dodson (North Light Books, 1985). Although really a series of exercises for the budding fine artist, this book contains many insights for rendering.

Architectural Presentation, by Chris Choate (Reinhold Book Corporation, 1961). Techniques for composing a rendering and creating mood with lighting and color are brilliantly explained and illustrated. It has been out of print for a decade, so look for this one at the library.

Selling Your Graphic Design and Illustration, by Tad Crawford and Arie Kopelman (St. Martin's Press, 1981). If you want to become a freelance architectural illustrator, you must learn to wear two hats: artist and businessperson. Self-promotion, contracts, billing and collections, taxes, and copyright law are all thoroughly covered to help you develop your business abilities.

Product Rendering with Markers, by Mark Arends (Van Nostrand Reinhold, 1985). The author conveys his mastery of rendering a variety of materials—such as chrome, brass, wood, and plastic— with lots of demonstrations and examples.

Perspective Grid Sourcebook, by Ernest Burden (Van Nostrand Reinhold, 1991). These computer generated grids are great as an underlay for quick freehand sketches.

Photographing Your Artwork, by Russell Hart (North Light Books, 1987). A detailed guide to photographing your artwork with a 35mm camera.

Atlas of Human Anatomy for the Artist, by Stephen Rogers Peck (Oxford University Press, 1951). When you decide to get serious about studying the structure and proportions of the human body, reach for this classic text.

Drawing on the Artist Within, by Betty Edwards (Simon and Schuster, 1986). Each of us is born with amazing, intuitive design and drawing ability, which Betty Edwards will help you unlock with a fascinating series of exercises. When you feel your creative juices waning, dip into these pages.

Marker Rendering Techniques, by Dick Powell and Patricia Monahan (North Light Books, 1987). This British import has excellent coverage of markers as a medium for advertising comps and illustration.

Decorating Rich, by Teri Seidman and Sherry Suib Cohen (Villard Books, 1988). A helpful reference for understanding the way residential designers create different "looks" for interiors—important when you are trying to find the right accessories and details to complete an interior concept sketch.

Color Drawing, by Michael E. Doyle (Van Nostrand Reinhold, 1981). The marker/colored pencil rendering style is a time-tested technique that is thoroughly covered here.

Architectural Rendering Techniques, by Mike W. Lin (Van Nostrand Reinhold, 1985). A portfolio of renderings in different styles and media.

Drawing the Future, by Paul Stevenson Oles (Van Nostrand Reinhold, 1988). This retrospective of a decade's work by one of the most well-known architectural renderers in America offers numerous insights.

Architectural Sketching in Markers, by Harold Linton and Roy J. Strickfaden (Van Nostrand Reinhold, 1991). A large portfolio of sketches and notes by an accomplished architectural artist and teacher.

GRAY SCALE STRIPS

Cut along dotted lines to create eight gray-scale strips

| 10% GRAY | 10% GRAY | 10% GRAY | 10% GRAY | 10% GRAY | 10% GRAY | 10% GRAY | 10% GRAY |

| 20% GRAY | 20% GRAY | 20% GRAY | 20% GRAY | 20% GRAY | 20% GRAY | 20% GRAY | 20% GRAY |

| 30% GRAY | 30% GRAY | 30% GRAY | 30% GRAY | 30% GRAY | 30% GRAY | 30% GRAY | 30% GRAY |

| 40% GRAY | 40% GRAY | 40% GRAY | 40% GRAY | 40% GRAY | 40% GRAY | 40% GRAY | 40% GRAY |

| 50% GRAY | 50% GRAY | 50% GRAY | 50% GRAY | 50% GRAY | 50% GRAY | 50% GRAY | 50% GRAY |

| 60% GRAY | 60% GRAY | 60% GRAY | 60% GRAY | 60% GRAY | 60% GRAY | 60% GRAY | 60% GRAY |

| 70% GRAY | 70% GRAY | 70% GRAY | 70% GRAY | 70% GRAY | 70% GRAY | 70% GRAY | 70% GRAY |

| 80% GRAY | 80% GRAY | 80% GRAY | 80% GRAY | 80% GRAY | 80% GRAY | 80% GRAY | 80% GRAY |

| 90% GRAY | 90% GRAY | 90% GRAY | 90% GRAY | 90% GRAY | 90% GRAY | 90% GRAY | 90% GRAY |

ILLUSTRATORS & DESIGNERS
featured in this book

Conrad Booker
Artefak Design
1238 Callowhill Street, #401
Philadelphia, PA 19103
215-925-5707

Michael Borne, AIA
Selzer Associates
1300 Skyway Tower, Southland Ctr.
400 North Olive
Dallas, TX 75201
(214) 220-2121

James Cagle
Cagle Associates
2190 Nine Oaks Drive
Kennesaw, GA 30144
(404) 499-9469

Janet Campbell
78 Parker Avenue, No. 3
San Francisco, CA 94118
(415) 750-1330

Michael E. Doyle
Communication Arts Incorporated
1112 Pearl Street
Boulder, CO 80302
(303) 447-8202

James Earl
Earl Design
17 Parkview Drive
Hingham, MA 02043
(617) 749-7982

Michael G. Flynn
Design & Illustration
1715 27th Avenue
San Francisco, CA 94122
(415) 681-0729

Dan Harmon
Dan Harmon & Associates
2839 Paces Ferry Road, Suite 370
Atlanta, GA 30339
(404) 436-0854

Eric Hyne
Art & Illustration
525 Maple Ridge Lane
Odenton, Maryland 21113
(301) 551-5405

Jack Juratovic, AFAS
2826 Aurora Drive
Lake Orion, MI 48360
(313) 391-0343

Bob McAllen
Illustrator
3268 Military Avenue
West Los Angeles, CA 90034
(213) 477-8374

Richard McGarry / Greg Madsen
McGarry & Madsen
Business Graphics
923 Lincoln Road
Miami Beach, FL 33139
(305) 674-0075

Syd Mead
Syd Mead, Inc.
1716 North Gardner
Los Angeles, CA 90046
(213) 850-5225

Richard Radke
Radke-Voss Collaborative
7233 West Touhy Avenue
Chicago, IL 60648
(312) 774-3525

Barbara Worth Ratner
Architectural Illustration
828 Charles Allen Drive, N.E.
Atlanta, GA 30308
(404) 876-3943

Samuel C. Ringman
Design & Illustration
2700 Fairmount Street, Suite 100
Dallas, TX 75201
(214) 871-9001

Akira Sato, AIA
The BJSS Group
320 West Bay Drive, Suite 212
Olympia, WA 98502
(206) 943-4650

Roy J. Strickfaden
Architect
25395 McAllister
Southfield, MI 48034
(313) 357-0505

Anthony Suminski
Architectural Renderings
933 East Clarke Street
Milwaukee, WI 53212
(414) 374-6018

Jerry Szwed
Lynn Wilson Associates
116 Alhambra Circle
Coral Gables, FL 33134
(305) 442-4041

Voytek Szczepanski
Voytek Designs, Inc.
104 Royal Park Drive, #3G
Fort Lauderdale, FL 33309
(305) 485-2528

Rene Thibault
Thibault Illustrators Ltd.
407 - 1509, Centre Street S.W.
Calgary, Alberta T2G 2E6
(403) 262-4383

Ace Torre
Design Consortium, Ltd.
5005 Magazine Street
New Orleans, LA 70115
(504) 899-2932

INDEX

When I am working on a problem,
I never think about beauty.
I think only of how to solve the problem.
But when I have finished,
if the solution is not beautiful,
I know it is wrong.

- Buckminster Fuller

COLOPHON

The text in this book was set in Minion, a contemporary digital type family created by designer Robert Slimbach. Inspired by the classic old–style typefaces of the late Renaissance, it incorporates the aesthetic and functional qualities that make text type inviting and easy to read.

Frutiger, a sans serif face designed in 1968 by Adrian Frutiger, was used for headlines and captions. It was originally created as a signage alphabet for the Charles de Gaulle Airport outside Paris.

The book title and question numbers were set in Kabel, chosen as an alternate sans serif face for its graphic character, and page layouts were composed with Quark Xpress 3.0 on an Apple Macintosh IIsi computer.